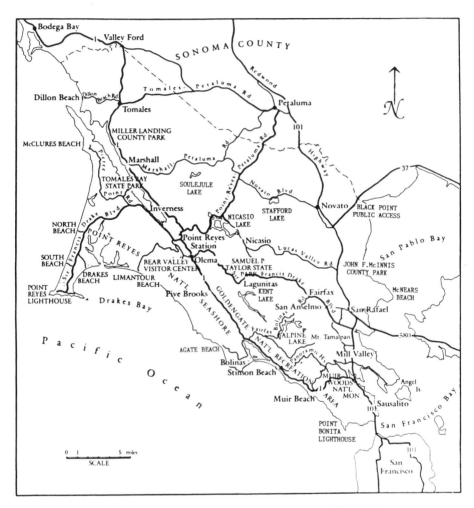

Map by *Dewey Livingston*

POINT BONITA
TO POINT REYES

OUTDOORS IN MARIN

61 PLACES TO VISIT

By DICK MURDOCK

Photographs & Captions by
Jayne Murdock

PREFACE: Dr. William Filante   **FOREWORD:** Beth Ashley

FIRST PRINTING, January 1989
SECOND PRINTING, January 1992

Some material in this book originally appeared in the Marin Independent Journal as outdoors columns by Dick Murdock and are presented here with permission

Library of Congress Catalog Card Number 88-26633
International Standard Book Number 0-932916-14-7

Library of Congress Cataloging-in-Publication Data

Murdock, Dick, 1917 -
    Point Bonita to Point Reyes.

    Bibliography: p.
    Includes index.
1. Marin County (Calif.)—Description and travel—
Guide-books.   2. Outdoor recreation—California—Marin
County—Guide-books.   I. Title.
F868.M3M8   1989   917.94'620453   88-26633
ISBN 0-932916-14-7

Published by
MAY-MURDOCK PUBLICATIONS
Drawer 1346 - 90 Glenwood Avenue
Ross California 94957

Printed in the United States of America

DEDICATION

To the memory of Jack Mason,
1912 – 1985
"The Point Reyes Historian"
author, protector, recorder of all things Marin
and our warm friend and mentor

"… A goodly country and fruitful
soil stored with many blessings
fit for the use of man."

from *The World Encompassed*
by Sir Francis Drake, 1628

Lagoon at Kehoe Beach

PREFACE

I believe a word of warning to the reader is in order. Proceed at your risk! This book is not toxic — it is only intoxicating in its beauty and subtlety. *Point Bonita to Point Reyes: Outdoors in Marin* is not your average pictorial book with all the natural highlights of the area, the spectacular formations and the numerous features that can only be found here in Marin. We do have these, but in addition you'll find the details, the history and politics that make Marin come alive before you.

And this is your risk, since you will not be able to stop at just reading the book. You will want to explore the famous and spectacular as well as the not so famous features that you read about here. And you will want to learn more of our history, politics and environment to find how it all comes together with the local government entities, city, county and special districts, as well as state and federal governments all working together to keep Marin the beautiful place it is.

Thus, this is a special book about a special place and special people. The kind of people, for example, who will design a house with a picture window not to frame the view of Mount Tam off in the distance, but rather to take in the large oak tree right outside the window so that you are a part of the great outdoors whether you are out on the deck or inside looking out. The kind of people who assess themselves to preserve the open hills around them as did the Lucas Valley residents and others who have since followed their example.

Fortunately, for most visitors to Marin, their greeting is a spectacular one across the Golden Gate Bridge. Perhaps, they will exit immediately and circle under and back to the hill overlooking the Bridge, explore old gun emplacements, and be awed by the sight of the Golden Gate and the Bay counties from above, a view that most people never see. Similarly, the Sausalito you experience is much more than the shops and bay vistas since it also has the Corps of Engineers' Bay-Delta Model, a testimonial to big Federal government, big water projects, and more recently, major efforts to improve the environment of the Bay.

Another typical Marin uniqueness is the Larkspur Landing area where our sleek Golden Gate ferries rub shoulders with scores of wind surfers who seem to venture far too close to San Quentin Prison as well as to ferries in the channel.

Of course, we also have our more typical sights like the Bon Air bike path and VitaCourse which combines the traffic jam of bikers, hikers, joggers and bird watchers (try to find the terns, egrets and herons which frequent these environs) with the usual number of Walkman tape recorders. When you hike around Phoenix Lake you will find that the water district maintains this as a scenic area, not for water supply, and rebuilt the dam because of earthquake danger, rather than tear it down and lose the lake.

West Marin is probably even more history. Soulajule Lake, for example, is the result of the water shortages in the 1970s. Out in Bear Valley, you actually walk along the earthquake fault part of the 1906 quake. You will also want to spend some time at Audubon Canyon Ranch which offers, for several months in the spring and summer of each year, close-up views of nesting herons and egrets, their carefully tended eggs and fledgling young. Uniquely Marin, the ranch regularly draws such a large crowd at their Mother's Day barbeque you have to stand in line for a telescope view of these nests.

The great expanse of the National Seashore has to draw you to the beaches and to the controversy of just where did Sir Francis Drake land on that voyage hundreds of years ago. You'll have plenty of time to contemplate such questions on your choice of spectacular, sweeping, and mostly isolated beaches that make up much of Marin's western edge. These are a dramatic contrast to Stinson Beach which draws thousands of people on a typical summer weekend making Marin look for the moment deceptively like many California locations.

Point Bonita to Point Reyes will help you learn and understand so much about Marin that you will surely come away with only one "stereotype" — namely that Marin does have a little bit of everything (well-run cities, national corporate headquarters, high-tech industry, flourishing agriculture, commuters, workers, rich, poor, centers of higher education, flourishing arts) but Marin also has a lot of things that make it special with its wilderness, beaches, mountains, lakes, forests, and a people who are in love with the environment, in the midst of one of the most exciting metropolitan areas in the world.

Bill Filante, M.D.
Assemblyman, 9th District
California State Legislature
San Rafael, California
August 1988

FOREWORD

When friends visit from another part of the country — or better yet — from another part of the world — I can feel my smugness grow for weeks before they arrive.

I'm perfectly prepared to give them the obligatory tour of Chinatown and (sigh!) Fisherman's Wharf, and I know they will be thrilled when we drive through the tunnel and The Bridge hits us smack in the eye. These are the sights they have come here to see. These are the sights on the postcards, the listings in each written guide.

But when they've seen all that — North Beach, Union Square, The Crookedest Street in the World — I'll be waiting to show them Marin.

The best part of having visitors is knocking their socks off with a trip to Point Reyes.

They already know that San Francisco is one of the world's great cities. What they can't believe is the proximity of one of the world's great wildernesses.

They are always amazed that they can drive through San Francisco — past the grand new hotels and the grand old Victorians, the elegant stores and the steep gleaming faces of skyscrapers — and stand, half an hour later, in the primeval stillness of Muir Woods.

Even those who live here pinch themselves.

Other parts of the world have knockout homes and great views and celebrity residents. Other suburban areas combine county living with urban pleasures — art, music, fabulous restaurants.

Other counties even have ferries.

But who has the Verna Dunshee Trail on the rim of Mount Tam? Kule Loklo and the Earthquake Trail at Bear Valley? Point Reyes Lighthouse when the whales are migrating south?

We have lakes and cows and beaches, wild mountains and surf, giant farms and hills of golden grass.

We have, in short, the great outdoors.

In *Point Bonita to Point Reyes*, Dick and Jayne Murdock celebrate that side of Marin and take us on a guided tour of its treasures.

They give us — in this beautifully designed book — a taste of what to see.

Few people have spent as much time exploring Marin, and few people have written about it more lovingly.

Since 1981, Dick — an ex-railroad engineer and a man in love with fishing — has had a weekly outdoor column in the *Marin Independent Journal.* Nearly two years ago, he added a second — a Sunday column — for the Marin at Play page. Each week he visits a different park or hiking trail or fishing hole, and tells his readers what he finds.

He and Jayne have been to places most of us haven't seen, and have taken a fresh look at ones we mistakenly thought we knew well.

How long has it been since you went crabbing at Fort Baker, picnicked at Paradise Park, or explored tidepools at Agate Beach?

How long has it been since you've pondered the history of Papermill Creek, or viewed a miniature marine ecosystem at the San Francisco Bay Model?

How long since you've gone up Mount Tam — for the view?

The beauty of this book, a collection of Dick's columns, is to remind us again what's at hand.

Dick is a good reporter, and a good writer: He tells us what we need to know and inspires us to find out more on our own.

Jayne's photographs just add to our joy.

Their affection for Marin County shines on every page, — leading old timers like me to smack our brows with delight.

Dick and Jayne are quick to say that this book only scratches the surface of the places to see.

But it's a terrific start.

The next time I have visitors due, I'll pick it up. Right after China Town and Union Square, I'll show them the glories of Marin. I'll give them their choice: Audubon Canyon Ranch? Phoenix Lake? Old artillery emplacements at the edge of the Golden Gate?

And I'll feel smug all over again.

Beth Ashley, Senior Lifestyles Writer
Marin Independent Journal
San Rafael, California
August 1988

INTRODUCTION

In researching and photographing places used in this book, Dick and I have become totally impressed with and enamored of the diverse and marvelous beauty of our county. Marin has been my home since 1924; Dick came here in 1974. We've always loved this place above all others. Now, added to our love, is a new dimension, a knowing. And we've become conscious of the great debt of gratitude we owe to those who had the vision to dream of preserving these wonders, and to those with the strength to fight to make the dreams reality.

Many mornings in these last months, with a list of five, six or — once — seven, places in hand, a picnic lunch packed, off we'd go on a photographic safari.

What riches! What treasure! Far from the HWY 101 corridor (it takes a surprisingly short time, in some cases, to get far away), we'd be in forests, glens, broad meadows, parks, playing fields, hillsides, ridges, moors, or beaches, beside a stream, creek, lake, pond, bay, lagoon or ocean. "Look at that!" I'd say to Dick. "Look at that!" he'd say around another curve in the road.

It wasn't just the places on our list; it was the getting to and from, and in between. With the wide green stretches of the Golden Gate National Recreation Area, and Point Reyes National Seashore, the watershed lands of the Marin Municipal Water District, national monuments, state parks and preserves, county, city and town parks, a wonderful amount of Marin is open space.

Views, from spectacular and overwhelming to serene and private, challenged our eyes and our camera. How to catch the world in a lens for a 3 x 5 black and white photo?

And our mountain, beloved Tamalpais, visible from all parts of the county — except deep canyons and the distant moors of West Marin, how special she is. In several cases, I had to choose not to show that familiar silhouette in the book: Five pictures in a row, would, I felt, be a bit redundant!

Each of the 61 places we picked, from the 80 plus columns Dick has written for the Marin at Play page of the Sunday *Marin Independent Journal,* was edited and adapted to a format more suitable for the permanency of a book. Often this involved additional research and another visit to the spot. And three times we returned to Muir Woods, trying for a better picture.

For each place we've covered, two more are begging to be done! Another day, another book, who knows? The list grows; the Sunday columns keep coming.

In the meantime, we hope you enjoy *Point Bonita to Point Reyes* as much as we relished the exciting task of creating it. And we hope you find as much pride and delight in visiting these places as we did.

Jayne May Murdock
Ross, California
August 1988

Tennessee Valley

CONTENTS

Point Bonita Lighthouse

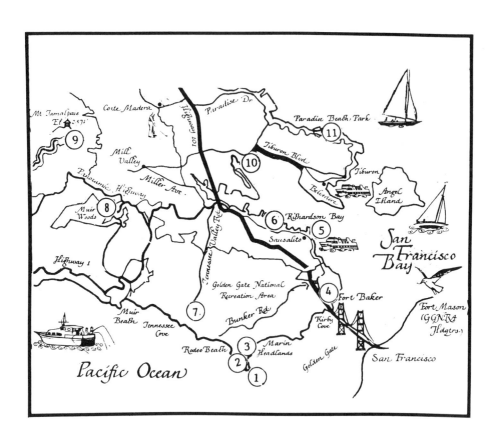

SOUTHERN MARIN

1   –   Point Bonita Lighthouse

2   –   Battery Mendell

3   –   Battery Wallace & Picnic Area

4   –   Fort Baker Fishing Pier

5   –   Sausalito Seawall

6   –   Bay Model, Sausalito

7   –   Tennessee Valley, Mill Valley

8   –   Muir Woods

9   –   Top of Mount Tamalpais

10   –   Richardson Bay Audubon Center

11   –   Paradise Park, Tiburon

POINT BONITA LIGHTHOUSE

through a tunnel, over a bridge

I F YOU LIKE spectacular beauty and adventure as part of your out-door life, visit Point Bonita Lighthouse on Marin Headlands. A sign just beyond the parking area reads "CLOSED" (which means, we discovered later, if no docents are on hand, the iron gate at the tunnel entrance is locked.) The sign also warns that a strenuous four-tenths of a mile hike awaits you. However, most weekends, the gate will be open with a volunteer or two to answer questions. It was windy, clear and cool the Sunday my wife, Jayne, and I made the tour.

The descending path is steep with San Francisco Bay on your left, open ocean to the right. "Hazardous cliffs — please stay on trail," a sign warns. So precipitous and rugged is the terrain, we were happy to comply. Then we walked through the tunnel chiseled out of solid rock by hand in 1875. That was the year before the lighthouse, built in 1855 on the cliff above, was moved to its present location.

Just beyond we met a volunteer docent with a counter. "You're numbers 98 and 99," she said. "If you hurry, there'll still be someone at the lighthouse. He'll show you some great old pictures. We'll be locking the gate soon."

Strung high above the rocky coastline, the suspension bridge spans a steep chasm and is limited to five people at a time. You can clearly hear the husky rumble of waves crashing against cliffs far below, and feel the wind as you make your way across.

The docent at the lighthouse that day was a volunteer from Greenbrae who tells interesting stories. "The bridge you just crossed was built in 1954," he said. "Waves reached the lighthouse in the storm of '87."

We looked at old photos, felt the atmosphere created by the sturdy old structure and imagined how life here must have been years ago. Today the lighthouse harbors a 1000-watt bulb that can be seen 18 miles at sea.

Only 10 more folks made the hike before the gate was closed and locked for the day. We braced ourselves for the hard climb out. Impressive views at every turn seem to make it easier. At least, they are a reason to pause and catch your breath! We will long remember this adventure. So will you.

For tour information call (415) 331-1540.

Looking down on Point Bonita lighthouse from the big turnaround beyond Battery Mendell, showing rocky shoreline in foreground, the opening of the Golden Gate and the cliffs south of San Francisco fading into the mist.

BATTERY MENDELL

2

spectacular view & a walk on the roof of history

V ISIT HISTORIC Point Bonita Lighthouse in Golden Gate National Recreation Area during the week and it may be closed. But don't despair. There's more to see right there any day of the week, or year, than you can imagine. Simply drive the short distance past Battery Mendell to the gravelled turnaround, park, get out and look.

Before your eyes is a sweeping 300-degree view that's hard to believe. If the day is clear, the circular vista stretches from Point Reyes in the north, closer to Bolinas Point, then edges down the coast to Muir Beach, Rodeo Beach and Lagoon. Directly below is Bird Island. Depending upon the time of year, you may see western gulls, cormorant and brown pelicans plus others. Straight out to sea are the Farallons, often invisible but always intriguing.

Then gaze left and look down at Point Bonita lighthouse. See waves crashing against rocky cliffs and watch the powerful light relentlessly and slowly switching on and off, regardless of the weather, to warn ships far at sea. And to the south, cliffs jutting into the ocean as far as Pacifica.

Complete your arc by taking in what can be seen of the Golden Gate Bridge and beyond, the silhouette of the San Francisco skyline — a breathtaking panorama.

As you leave, stop to explore Battery Mendell on your right. Ghost soldiers from wars far past seem just behind the barred windows, walking in the strong cement cubicles. Two emplacements, guns long gone, now resemble amphitheaters with circular steps for seating.

This hefty reinforced installation bears the name of Army engineer Colonel George H. Mendell, who designed it against and into a hill to be invisible from the sea. In operation from 1905-43, it featured two unique disappearing guns which folded back after firing.

Now you can climb the outside stairs, walk on the grassy roof. And for the outdoor lover, here you have challenging country, fantastic views, clean air, and great hiking for all the exercise you need.

The exposed front of Battery Mendell taken from across the road. The installation was built into the bluff to be invisible from the sea. Now grass grows on the roofs, and ghosts of artillery men seem to inhabit the barred and boarded rooms.

BATTERY WALLACE & PICNIC AREA

3

another tunnel & a backward look at the bridge

G OLDEN GATE National Recreation Area's Battery Wallace and adjacent windswept picnic grounds certainly qualify as places to visit by those who love history and views.

There's ample parking, particularly during the week. Be sure to give Battery Wallace a thorough inspection and let your mind drift back to 1919 when it was an open-firing platform that held huge guns with a range of 17 miles. In 1942 it was cemented over as protection against aerial attack and remains that way today.

A unique, mysterious cement tunnel takes you past dark blockaded doorways to your left. They once led to underground storage rooms and crew quarters.

When through the tunnel, look around. Across a chasm you'll see Battery Mendell, another fortification worth a visit (see previous article.)

Battery Wallace was declared obsolete in 1948 but remains an installation of historical significance.

Across the road is a grassy picnic area with six sturdy tables and barbeque grills. A grove of cypress trees is nearby in the event you need shade. From here, looking east, the south tower of the Golden

Gate Bridge is visible with the San Francisco skyline silhouetted beyond. This is a popular knoll on sunny weekends.

Down a fire lane, way below, is a walk-in campground. More secluded and quite sheltered, it offers a different outlook. Call (415) 331-1540 for reservations.

Should you choose to walk, take it easy so not to miss any of the fantastic Marin Headlands scenery. There are many trails to other points of interest in the Golden Gate National Recreation Area. If you have a good parking spot near Battery Wallace, leave your car there and take your time walking around Point Bonita. This breathtaking spot is filled with history as well as beauty. What better outdoor therapy? Try it.

Picnic with a view, a perfect spot on a clear windless day. Across the road is Battery Wallace, then on up the hill to the parking lot for the lighthouse.

FORT BAKER FISHING PIER

4

free angling on marin's doorstep

F ORT BAKER, BENEATH the north portal of the Golden Gate Bridge, is an idyllic setting for many things. Rich in military history, the complex is a fine place for bicyclists, picnickers, hikers, joggers, nature lovers, photographers and anglers.

I first went there a few years ago researching an article for a magazine, and came away deeply impressed. I've been back many times since.

Established in 1897, Baker is the oldest of three forts on the Marin Headlands which once guarded the Golden Gate with big guns and later with Nike missiles.

Now part of the Golden Gate National Recreation Area, a single visit there underscores another of Marin's special places — one for sheer relaxation and enjoyment.

On a clear day the San Francisco skyline is silhouetted across the bay in an ever-changing pattern of light and shadow, impressive and unforgettable. Many breathtaking and memorable photos have been taken from various spots around Fort Baker.

The old L-shaped military wharf at Horseshoe Bay now serves as a fine public fishing pier. No license is required and you can use two rods with no more than three hooks each, or one rod and one crab net.

Those using trout tackle, 6-pound test line and No. 6 or 8 hooks are in for some fun catching sand sole, a variety of perch, and jacksmelt when they're running. However, heavy saltwater gear is better if you're after salmon, striped bass, halibut, rays or sturgeon. The most popular baits are pile worms, anchovies, grass shrimp, ghost and mud shrimp. Bullheads and mudsuckers are good when in quest of striped bass.

Fishing is also permitted off the breakwater that protects the yacht harbor, and off rocky points in either direction. However, here you do need a current angling license in your possession.

To get there take the Alexander Avenue turnoff, bear left at the GGNRA sign and then, just before the tunnel to Cronkhite, swing right on Bunker Road and head down to Fort Baker.

For more information call (415) 561-3870 or 561-3995.

Shot from almost under the north tower of Golden Gate Bridge, a view of the L-shaped fishing pier at Fort Baker, with Alcatraz at the right and the East Bay hills on the horizon. Road in the foreground goes under the bridge and joins the one that leads to the headlands.

SAUSALITO SEAWALL

5

rugged rocks, lapping waves — a bayfront saved

S AUSALITO OWES MUCH of its charm as a fishing spot to geography and some timely legislation," wrote Mike Hayden in his book, *Pier Fishing on San Francisco Bay.*

Anglers know that this quaint town is more than steep hills, impressive homes, boutiques, restaurants and arts and crafts shops. There are also wharves, marinas, mini-parks and a long stretch of seawall interrupted only once by restaurants.

Thanks to the McAteer-Petris Act of 1965, there is public access to the waterfront and fishing at several places off Bridgeway Boulevard, the town's main street.

Almost always there are anglers lined up along the seawall fishing for perch, rays, shark and jacksmelt when they're running. Particularly exciting is a good herring run when people can net them off the seawall. Unfortunately, there have been few good runs in recent years. This could change any winter.

Again I quote from Mike Hayden's book: "Within minutes after the local grapevine signals the arrival of a herring run, the docks and seawall become lined elbow-to-elbow with people furiously working dip nets."

Should a herring run develop, it would be in late December so be on the alert around that time of year.

Often you can see hundreds of baby crabs scurrying around, over and under those big rocks at the water's edge, retreating from the shadow you cast as you walk along.

Weathered, backless wood benches and attractive hexagonal concrete trashcan holders are placed at intervals along the sidewalk above the seawall.

The seawall pathway below the sidewalk ends where two popular restaurant buildings jut out over the bay. Beyond, the seawall continues, with no path, for a short distance, ending at a small pavilion. Here a plaque dedicates the tiny park to Yee Tock Chee, a kindly Oriental who lived from 1891 to 1975, operated Marin Fruit Company across the street and was known for helping those in need.

For the latest information about fishing at Sausalito, call (415) 332-1015.

Standing midway on the seawall, where steps lead down from the sidewalk, looking south. Just to the left and out of the picture is a sculptured sea lion by local artist, Al Sebrian, which stands in the bay a few feet offshore.

BAY MODEL

6

an indoor look at the great outdoors

L OVERS OF San Francisco Bay and the delta can enhance their knowledge of this great eco-system by visiting the Bay Model, 2100 Bridgeway Boulevard, Sausalito.

The large waterfront building, originally a Marinship warehouse during World War II, houses a one-acre scale model of San Francisco Bay and the Sacramento-San Joaquin delta. This fascinating layout, operated by the United States Army Corps of Engineers, can keep you spellbound for hours. You get an impressive overview of both familiar and unfamiliar locales. Here is a great place to study water movement patterns, shoaling, pollution, salinity. Computer-generated tides and currents raise and drop water levels. Operation of the model is dependent on the engineering staff's schedule.

The entire complex is far more than a giant topographical floor map. It is a working laboratory where engineers study the impact of physical changes on the bay and delta. That the operation also provides visitors, scientists and educators with valuable information and a chance to view the complete bay-delta system from above is a delightful and beautifully planned by-product.

Here you can learn the historical, environmental and cultural aspects of our region. There's a large exhibit area of maps, glass-enclosed ship models, and a Bay Model scrap book with pictures that tell the unique story.

A genial volunteer from San Anselmo was on hand to answer questions. "The first stage was built about 1958," he said, "the delta, from mid to late '60s. The Visitor Center opened in 1981 with ramps, exhibits and stations allowing self-viewing. We book guided tours for groups of 10 or more."

Upstairs is an engrossing room, the Pool of Life. From there you can walk outside to a bay overlook with a great view of the Marin hills and Mount Tamalpais. Fishing vessels and other ships are tied up along the waterfront. Prominent is the Wapana, last of the steam schooners, listing as she awaits her fate.

A staircase leads down to restrooms, picnic tables, flower basins, and a big parking area.

For more information call (415) 332-3870 or 3871.

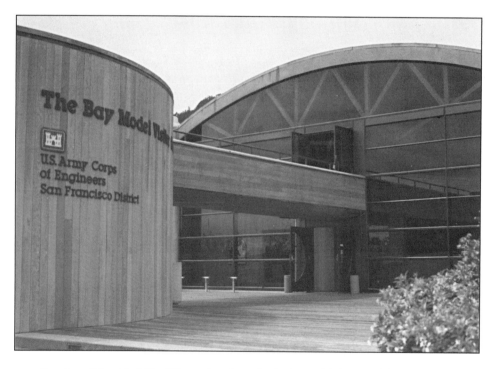

Exterior of Bay Model building taken from dock where old ships and fishing boats are moored. The circular structure on the left houses restrooms and stairway to second deck ramp.

TENNESSEE VALLEY

7

over hill & dale to the sea

F YOU'VE NEVER visited Tennessee Valley, here's a worthwhile out-door experience, easily accessible and, once experienced, difficult to forget.

The two-mile walk to the sea from the dirt parking area and horse corrals at the end of Tennessee Valley Road, off HWY One in Mill Valley, is an adventure for hikers, joggers, bikers, birders, runners and nature lovers.

Start down the gentle grade on a paved road or on the dirt trail to the left near a eucalyptus grove. No pets allowed. The path goes through grasslands and chaparral with steep hills on either side. The first junction leads to Haypress walk-in camp on your right. The early spring day we were there, a dad and his two tykes made a couple of trips in, pulling a red wagon loaded with camping goods. Just beyond is Fox Trail and a plant restoration area. The pavement ends at the private ranch house on the left.

Now the path skirts a seasonally babbling creek bordered by ferns, willows and an occasional cypress, with splashes of color from a broad spectrum of wildflowers.

Walking is easy with much to see. When the road splits, bear left toward Tennessee Beach, named after the 1853 shipwreck of the *S.S. Tennessee*. Soon the surf is heard and the breeze carries a whiff of cool salt-tinged air. When you pass a giant old pine on the left, a red cabin and corrugated iron shed to the right, you're about halfway to the ocean.

Soon you cross the Pacific Coast Trail. Signs point toward Rodeo Beach three miles to the south, Muir Beach the same distance north. Sea breezes are more pronounced as you pass a hitching post, latrine, and trash barrel, and then skirt a freshwater lagoon. Now the sound of a crashing surf is clear and in a short time you reach a small horse-shoe-shaped dark sand beach.

There's a bench high on a bluff to the north, with stairs climbing even higher up the slope toward a natural cave slicing through the hill's rocky crest.

To the south, miniature Gibraltars jut from the sea seeming imper-vious to the relentless pounding of the everlasting waves. Such an intriguing place! There are people around, but you don't notice. Instead, you sit and absorb the wonder, reluctant to even think about starting back.

At the beginning of the walk to the sea. Ahead the path curves around and passes between two hills. Haypress walk-in campground is off to the right.

31

MUIR WOODS

a walk under trees that humble

8

I S MUIR WOODS — one of the most popular tourist attractions in Marin — with the longest possible string of restrictions, worth the hassle to visit? No picnicking or camping on this 580 acres, pets are not permitted, motorized equipment, horses and bicycles are prohibited. Crowds around the Visitor's Center are often overwhelming, particularly on weekends and during summer months. Parking is a muddle. Is what's left enough to make it worthwhile?

Absolutely! A visit here is unforgettable. These very restrictions preserve the best in Marin's unique national monument. Planning and foresight went into protecting this beautiful area, along Redwood and Fern creeks, for future generations. In fact, the summer of 1988 found authorities weighing various plans to impose more rules and restrictions. We are, it seems, in danger of loving our beloved trees to death!

Redwoods of all sizes dominate the woods. The tallest tree here is 250 feet, the widest 13.5 feet, with many close contenders. Ferns are abundant. Besides redwoods, there are red alders, Douglas firs, bay, and oaks plus wild rhododendron, azalea, hazelnut and delicate flowers. Watch for wildlife, especially in the remote reaches of the park.

Many don't wander that far, too overwhelmed by their initial sight of the primeval forest, the informative signs, the paved trails, the sheer tranquil beauty of the canyon, the milling masses. Watching awed visitors, hearing them exclaim in many languages and accents underscores the world-wide attraction of Muir Woods and the danger to the environment inherent therein.

Years ago the world-famed Mount Tamalpais and Muir Woods Railroad had a branch line that ran into the woods. The story, a fascinating one, is well told in *The Crookedest Railroad in the World* by Ted Wurm and Al Graves.

At the turn of the century, outdoorsman William Kent was persuaded by John Muir to buy the area and preserve it. Kent then donated the land to the federal government. As a result, in 1908, President Theodore Roosevelt proclaimed the woods a national monument.

A frequent visitor to Muir Woods, I've discovered the real secret is to keep walking. Soon you'll find yourself virtually alone among majestic redwoods, thanks to the foresight of these fine, farsighted gentlemen.

Dark is the canopy of these inspiring redwoods, rough bark and gentle leaves reflecting shafts of light that filter through. No picture can do justice to this special place. Look, live, feel the wonder here preserved for everyone, and be thankful to those with foresight... and to God.

MOUNT TAMALPAIS

9

a hike around our legendary lookout

E VERY MARINITE SHOULD periodically visit the top of Mount Tamalpais. Not to means missing an exhilarating outdoor experience. The view from here defies description and recreational opportunities abound — hiking, biking, picnicking, photography.

The Verna Dunshee trail circles the peak well below the lookout. By all means take the walk. Only seven-tenths of a mile, there are spectacular breathtaking views in every direction. Below, the old railroad grade with its famed Double Bow Knot which now serves as both fire road and hiking trail, resembles a brown serpent, snaking down the mountainside to Mill Valley.

Just before you complete your circuit, a steep, rocky path veers upward on the left. Half way up this two-tenths of a mile climb to Gardner Lookout at the mountain's peak — elevation 2571 feet — bear right for the steepest route to the structure. Otherwise, circle the peak on an easier grade with awesome panoramas at every turn. The largest Marin Water District lake you see far below is Bon Tempe, close to it, tiny Lagunitas. The strenuous hike to the lookout is worthwhile, even though the public is not allowed in the structure itself.

Gardner Lookout was dedicated May 9, 1937 to Edwin Burroughs Gardner, long-time chief warden of Tamalpais Forest Fire District who died in 1935.

Once back at the parking area, there are restrooms and plenty of space for picnicking with many other trails to hike. The air is great for breathing up here and even on hot days, cool in the shade of oaks, pine and bay.

On May Day 1988, Mt. Tamalpais Interpretive Association conducted a ribbon-cutting ceremony at East Peak Visitor Center. Following months of renovation, doors reopened to once again serve the community as the information base and source of history and lore of Mount Tamalpais State Park.

Volunteers, working with park rangers, refinished the center's interior. Now featured are murals and animal displays depicting the mountain's rich environmental habitat, past and present. Closed late in 1987 for the renovation, the center is now open on weekends only.

There's no way to forget the day you visit East Peak and walk around the top of our fabled mountain.

The little building shown above is the bump on the mountain's silhouette when viewed from a distance. Picture taken from stonewall at east end of parking lot. Spread out in every direction, except west, are views and vistas defying description. A walk on the path around the top, then up to the base of the lookout, will produce an entire scrapbook of rare sights.

RICHARDSON BAY
AUDUBON CENTER

window on nature

R ICHARDSON BAY Audubon Center and Sanctuary is a place for outdoor lovers to visit any Wednesday through Sunday.

True, about ten times more water than land is involved, which makes the location no less intriguing. In fact, the sanctuary is referred to as an "environmental education center — a window on the bay," providing habitat for thousands of migrating waterfowl.

Jayne and I were there one day early in April and came away feeling good about a spot so impressive, yet so close. From 11 onshore acres we clearly viewed the 900 wet ones, mostly for the birds. And they were there, to our delight, in full feathered force.

We found the air here brisk, salt-tinged, invigorating, the view stretching all the way to the San Francisco skyline.

The Victorian Lyford House with many distinctive features including a spiral staircase, gold leaf, etched glass, and a skylight fashioned from the windows of an old sailing ship, stands proudly on a bluff overlooking the bay. Built in the late 1870s by Dr. Benjamin Lyford who was considered an eccentric because of his ultra-hygienic Eagle Dairy, a forerunner of modern cleanliness, the elegant old home is now only open Sundays from 1-4 p.m. with guided tours.

Two curved cement benches overlooking Richardson Bay pay tribute to a pair of dedicated conservationists — Mrs. Rose Verral, who donated the property, and Caroline Livermore. Their influential efforts helped save this spot from developers.

Besides benches, there's a lookout and 32 stairs with a curved iron railing that lead down to beaches of dark pebbly sand and a rocky shoreline.

While there, be sure to walk the well-marked trails and visit the Book Nest, a store that offers everything from children's books to those for birders and environmentalists.

The facility is located at 376 Greenwood Beach Road, Tiburon. Park your car outside and walk in.

For more information call (415) 388-2524.

Lyford house from the driveway. Part of Richardson Bay bridge is visible. Stairs lead down the bluff to the beach, and behind the house, trails wander through cypress and eucalyptus to the hills and marshes beyond.

PARADISE BEACH PARK

sloping lawns, sandy beach & fishing pier

O F MARIN'S COUNTY parks, Paradise Beach ranks among the oldest and loveliest, a spot worth visiting at any time of year, but on crisp winter days, there's the added advantage of having plenty of room for parking, picnicking and fishing.

The 19-acre partially wooded complex has rolling green lawns, barbequing and picnic areas and a large T-shaped fishing pier with benches, tap water and fish sinks, and an impressive and sweeping view of the upper bay from the pier.

Years ago, before access roads, weekend boaters camped here to fish and enjoy the beach. It was a gathering spot for the affluent.

Now this beautiful place is for everybody.

Another favorable feature is its location on the lee side of the Tiburon Peninsula. Paradise Beach is so protected that prevailing winds are seldom strong enough to interfere with the enjoyment of anglers, loafers and picnickers.

During summer months when crowds converge on Paradise, the sandy beach gets heavy use. No pets here because of limited facilities. Large group picnics are by permit only.

Anglers can expect action if they play tides right, use likely baits and know the proper equipment. Some striped bass and a few sturgeon are taken each year, but the predominate species are perch, smelt and flounder. Using light equipment is a challenging experience that will tax your angling skills should you hook something big. This is quite possible since the pier's position is not too far from the north end of tide-torn Raccoon Strait where sturgeon, salmon, striped bass and halibut migrate at various times of the year.

If you've never visited Paradise Beach, late winter is a great time. You need only warm clothes, a sunny day, a picnic basket, and the joy of living. The latter comes automatically once you arrive.

To get there, traveling north or south on HWY 101, take the Tiburon turnoff, go a mile or so to Trestle Glen Boulevard, swing left for about the same distance. At the fire station, turn right on Paradise Drive.

For details of open hours and fees, call (415) 499-6387.

Looking down the curving paths and sloping lawns, a part of the fishing pier and a piece of the beach and barbeque facilities are visible. Restrooms are in middle of the picture. Taken in the fall when leaves were almost off the poplar trees.

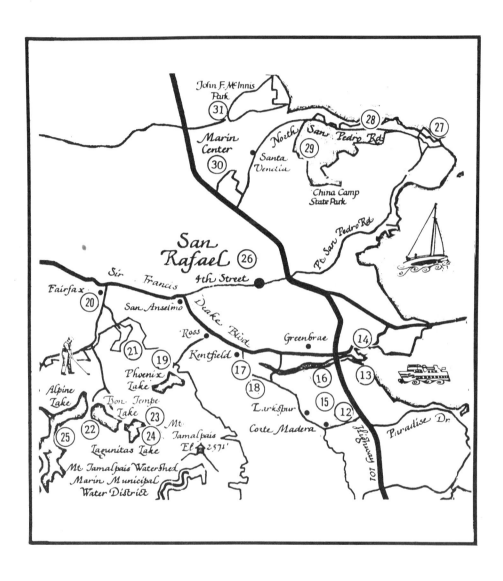

John F. McInnis Park
(31)

Marin Center
(30)

North San Pedro Rd.
(28)
(27)
(29)

Santa Venetia

China Camp State Park

Pt. San Pedro Rd.

San Rafael
(26)

Sir Francis
4th Street

Fairfax
(20)

San Anselmo

Drake Blvd.

Ross
(21)
(19)
Kentfield

Phoenix Lake

Greenbrae
(14)

(17)
(18)
(16)
(13)

Alpine Lake

Bon Tempe Lake
(23)

Larkspur
(15)
(12)

Corte Madera
Paradise Dr.

(25)
(22)
(24)
Lagunitas Lake

Mt. Tamalpais El. ▲ 2571'

Mt. Tamalpais Watershed
Marin Municipal
Water District

Highway 101

40

CENTRAL MARIN

12 – Corte Madera Town Park

13 – Last of the Corte Madera Marsh Lands

14 – Remillard Park, Larkspur Landing

15 – Marin Community Fields, Larkspur

16 – Piper Park, Larkspur

17 – Bon Air VitaCourse, Kentfield/Greenbrae

18 – Corte Madera Creek Fishing

19 – Phoenix Lake, MMWD

20 – Fairfax City Park

21 – Deer Park Picnic Area, Fairfax

22 – Bon Tempe Lake, MMWD

23 – Magnificent Madrone, MMWD

24 – Lagunitas Lake, MMWD

25 – Alpine Lake & Cataract Trail, MMWD

26 – Boyd Park, San Rafael

27 – McNear's Beach County Park, SR

28 – China Camp State Park, San Rafael

29 – Back Ranch Meadows, San Rafael

30 – Civic Center Lagoon, San Rafael

31 – McInnis City Park, San Rafael

CORTE MADERA TOWN PARK

—12

perfect place for picnic & play

TOWN PARK IN Corte Madera is an impressive 22-acre outdoor recreational complex.

It lies between Pixley and Eastman Avenues on Tamalpais Drive with ample parking and public restrooms off Pixley and again in the area of the Corte Madera Recreation Center building.

An abundance of large-lettered signs remind you that animals are prohibited, one of few restrictions at this neatly groomed park.

Eighteen parcourse outdoor fitness stations are placed at sensible intervals, each with an illustrated guide on how to perform a particular exercise. There are par ratings for those just starting exercise programs, those more sporting, as well as champions who are in superb physical condition.

Paved pathways, wide rolling close-cut lawns, trees and shrubs of many varieties and descriptions are always at hand to greet strollers, joggers, runners, picnickers and all others enjoying the beauty of this well-designed park.

An arched bridge crosses a slough at the eastern boundary. Access to a mini-shopping center is available to the south.

Neil Cummins School occupies the northeast corner with its playgrounds and athletic facilities.

Sports played here include tennis, handball, baseball, basketball, soccer and badminton. There are large and small playgrounds with rings, swings and slides and other forms of fun for youngsters.

Picnic and barbeque facilities are outstanding. Well-shaded tables are spotted beneath groves of redwood, fir, eucalyptus, pine and other sheltering trees. Even those convenient trash barrels are attractive.

True, no fishing's available here, but the Corte Madera Recreation Center building is where Keith Fraser's popular sturgeon-striper seminars are held each year.

Before departing Town Park, be sure to look west. There stands spectacular Mount Tamalpais, proudly guarding one of the county's nicest recreational facilities.

One small corner of the expansive and well-tended Town Park. It would take a collage to show all the facets of this place. Mount Tamalpais in background.

CORTE MADERA MARSHLAND

13

tules, seagulls & shore birds

THE LAST OF THE Corte Madera marshland has been preserved for nature, wildlife and outdoor lovers, thanks to those with foresight.

You can see the remaining treasure along old Redwood Highway in the mile between San Clemente Drive and Larkspur city limits. From HWY 101, take Lucky Drive turnoff, head south on Redwood until you come to a small paved six-car parking area on your left with three benches facing east. This is a fine place to start walking, jogging, running or biking. Or just to sit peacefully and observe the wildlife.

The pathway is wide and paved. Head south toward Corte Madera Village. Highway 101 is to your right for a few hundred yards until the frontage road abreast of you swings sharply left and becomes divided.

An impressive spread of boggy, tule-clad marshland reaches toward the bay on your left. As you progress southward, great views of the sloughs, bay, San Quentin and the Richmond-San Rafael Bridge are yours for the turning of a head. In fact, so wide open is it along here, fantastic scenes greet the eye in most directions, Marin at its best.

That large overflow roped-off parking area on the waterside becomes a collection of puddles when it rains and creates a massive convention center for gulls. At least a thousand occupied the puddles the day I enjoyed the two-mile roundtrip stroll from the six-car parking area to San Clemente Drive and back. There were few folks on the path that day — one runner and some bikers.

The route is partly landscaped in a natural manner. This is a productive location for birders. I saw many different winged creatures in this vast expanse of protected marsh. Signs constantly remind that dogs must be on a leash and no dumping is allowed.

Mount Tamalpais to the west is often obscured by clouds. Surrounding hills change color with the seasons. Each stop here is a new experience, a great place to get a bit of fresh air and exercise.

From the parking area, the shrinking marshland stretches out to the slough and, beyond, the bay. These benches are a grand observation spot from which to watch the many shore and waterbirds that congregate in the marsh.

REMILLARD PARK

ferry boats & wind surfers

I F YOU WANT some real outdoor atmosphere, don't bypass Remillard Park at Larkspur Landing.

Intriguing though that complex of shops is, it's not your destination. Instead, beyond the ferry complex, pull over where you can park by the side of the road. There's more to see here than you can imagine — long, black-topped paths and gravelled walkways lead a mile or more toward San Quentin with a multitude of surprises along the colorful route.

Starting across from Larkspur Ferry landing, beyond the mouth of Corte Madera Creek, just the opportunity to watch these sleek boats maneuver is worthwhile.

And walking, jogging, running, or birdwatching, you won't be able to keep your eyes off Mount Tamalpais. The view of the sleeping maiden from this vantage point is outstanding.

As you progress eastward along the surfaced walkway you'll come to Remillard Park's large pond. There's a sign that reads "Public Shore, No Dogs, Bikes." A gravelled levee divides the pond from the bay in a pleasing manner with benches and trash barrels along the way. Mallards, mudhens and perhaps some turtles sunning themselves, inhabit the pond. Other visitors and natives include a multitude of insects and marauding raccoons.

As the levee bends shoreward at the end, there is a pair of picnic tables, a drinking fountain, willows and eucalyptus trees, and a small parking area for cars. "A pond is a balanced habitat community," reads a convenient sign.

Remillard Park is comparatively new, an enhancement project funded by the State Coastal Conservancy, Marin Audubon Society and the City of Larkspur. The tall chimney of the old Remillard Brickyard, now a state historical landmark, is across Sir Francis Drake Boulevard and worth a look.

There's another bonus in store if it happens to be a windy day and the tide is high. Wind surfers — acrobatic athletes challenging nature to a duel on the water!

An unforgettable show, particularly when the estuary is full of sails. The thrills, spills and balancing acts are hard to believe, making it a great place for outdoors folks to spend a little leisure time.

With the airy ferry building and one of the boats at the dock off to the right, Mount Tamalpais, once again, in the background, and some of the many seagulls in sight, here is the start of Remillard Park. Down the path to the left is where you'll see the wind surfers.

MARIN COMMUNITY FIELDS

15

beep ball, running trail & other games

NOT LONG AFTER it was dedicated, I walked Marin Community Fields with Lynn Moody, wife of Henry Moody, a co-chairman of Community Field Association. I saw 17 well-groomed acres of playing fields and heard the happy shouts of participating athletes as Lynn explained how this impressive outdoor complex came into being.

"This is the result," she said, "of a great coordinated effort, private and public."

The parcel lies just south of Redwood High School and is operated by the Community Field Association. With the aid of $50,000 from the Buck Trust, grants and work donated by civic groups, private individuals and construction firms, the fields are now complete. Dedication ceremonies took place September 19, 1987.

"Let the games begin!" was the hue and cry of the Tamalpais District Board of Trustees, organizations, county and city agencies and everyone involved in helping to make Marin Community Fields a working reality.

This complex is more than just a number of playing fields. It's an architectural achievement meticulously designed to benefit the general public and students, and to support athletic competition in Marin County.

There is a sign dedicating the place to Beryl Buck, then comes the impressive Kreitzberg Amphitheater. Just beyond, the greens spread in a pleasing pattern, with berms of natural grass delineating them — Nave Fields Nos. 1 and 2 for softball; Cagwin and Dorward Field for soccer; Ghilotti Field, rugby; Moody Field for beep ball by the blind, and other outdoor games.

Don't overlook the Tamalpa running trail, a great place to keep in shape. Since the games have begun, this multi-purpose complex is being well used.

Mount Tamalpais again overlooks the fields in a benevolent manner, as if to compliment a great united effort.

"Applications are open," Lynn Moody said, "for rugby, soccer and softball."

For more information, phone (415) 924-2306.

The vastness of the green playing areas is lost in this picture. Just imagine it, stretching in all directions, each field with an appropriate backstop or goal, tournaments and games in progress. Redwood High School is to the right, HWY 101 a few blocks to your back.

PIPER PARK

16

spacious greens & well-groomed fields

IF YOU'RE A Marin sportsman and outdoor lover, likely you have, at some time, visited Larkspur's spacious Piper Park. If you haven't, better give it a whirl.

The impressive 26-acre spread at 250 Doherty Drive encompasses many recreational outlets including walking, jogging, running, softball, tennis, soccer, badminton, frisbee and about any other healthful activity you can think of.

Maintained by the Larkspur Park and Recreation Department, the place reflects care. Also, it's so well designed that those manicured rolling green lawns stand out, giving you a special feeling of open space in the midst of a populated urban area.

On the Saturday we visited, I found ample parking in the paved lot and roamed at will, fascinated that this complex is bordered by marsh and sloughs on three sides with a spectacular view of Mount Tamalpais to the west. A gentle gravelled path circumscribes the entire area.

I stopped at every one of the 15 Wells Fargo Gamefield stations, studying the posted exercise instructions. All were in place but No. 8, which had obviously been vandalized.

A fine playground for kids was in use, but only a few picnickers were utilizing the large section where tables are placed in a beckoning manner.

50

At the east boundary, the marsh is a wildlife sanctuary with no dogs allowed. Many shore birds were in sight.

Both softball fields and all four tennis courts were occupied. Still the facility seemed uncrowded. Not so, I understand, when baseball playoffs are in full swing.

Clean restrooms are available. Posted signs ask you to scoop up after your dog and animals must be leashed.

To the west, completing the circuit, there's a fenced community garden and a fine grassy field with a magnificent felled tree trunk backed by an artistic display of splendid rocks.

And, of course, the guardian saint of Marin's outdoors, Mount Tamalpais, serves as a benign backdrop.

Picture taken facing away from Mount Tamalpais for a change! Shown is one of the great play structures, a bit of the curving pathway and a sweep of green grass.

BON AIR VITACOURSE

creekside stations for healthy exercise

17

W HAT IS A Vitacourse?
Known by several names, parcourse being a popular one, the concept originated in Switzerland in the 1960s, and consists of a paved path with exercise stations at regular intervals.

Marin has several such courses. One of the most used parallels Corte Madera Creek between College Avenue in Kentfield and Larkspur city limits sign on Bon Air Road.

This one has 22 stations, each with illustrations and printed instructions on how to properly use without overdoing it. There are rings, bars and boards to assist with calisthenics. The course is a challenge to exercisers of all ages and the walkway itself offers a great deal to outdoor lovers.

On an overcast weekday morning I decided upon a closer look at the intriguing layout. Already numerous walkers, joggers, runners, cyclists, dog-walkers, birders and nature lovers were in evidence. Most gave me cheery greetings.

I started at College of Marin although parking is easier at the Marin General Hospital end. At first, I was west of the cement flood control channel, warned by signs to keep right. In a short while, the wide level paved path comes to Corte Madera Creek which is spanned by a wooden bridge with a protective cyclone fence.

Soon I passed College of Marin's ecology area on the left and a mini-park between stations 19 and 20. The cement channel has ended and the creek is now meandering through a marsh area. I spotted a white egret and a blue heron. Mount Tamalpais to the west was still cloud-shrouded. There are benches here and there for resting. If the tide is high, you may see an angler plugging for striped bass.

As you approach Bon Air Road, trails lead off at stops 14 and 9 across the marsh in an easterly direction. If you follow in sequence as directed, you'll cross little wooden bridges. Stations 11 and 12 are adjacent to Bon Air Road.

The course is a measured mile, two miles round trip. It's well worth the effort, an opportunity to enjoy Marin's beauty in a healthy manner.

Proximity to the changing tidal beauty of Corte Madera Creek makes this course unique. Whatever you're doing, you can also watch water birds in the creek and marshland.

CORTE MADERA CREEK

18

shore casting for stripers

I F YOU'RE A saltwater fisherman who doesn't care for boats, there are good bank fishing opportunities along Corte Madera Creek.

Casting lures from shore can be fun and productive. The same with bait fishing. Once you learn the spots, how and when to fish the tides, great action is likely to be experienced.

Fishing high changes seems most effective. One day I saw a lone angler on Corte Madera Creek behind the Pizza Hut on Bon Air Road. It was afternoon, the tide was in and this young fellow was casting a broken-back Rebel, retrieving the lure in jerks.

Suddenly his rodtip dipped and he fought a five-pound striper to the shore. He reached down, unhooked the lure and released the fish. Before I left, he hooked and released three more in short order!

Overcrowding is seldom, if ever, a problem when you chose to bank fish. Summer and fall are excellent times to toss lures at stripers. When fish are being taken in boats trolling close to shore, you, too, can reach them casting from land. It just might get exciting.

Several other access spots along Corte Madera Creek have proved productive: The bike path behind Zim's Restaurant; beneath HWY 101; near Larkspur Landing ferry slips and beyond toward San Quentin.

Time proven lures include Rebels, Kastmasters, 1/2-ounce Worm-Tail Jigs, Hair Raisers, Pet Spoons and others. Bait anglers prefer pile worms, anchovies, grass, ghost or mud shrimp. Bullheads and mud-suckers are also used.

For sport, I prefer trout gear with six-pound test line, but this can get you in trouble if a large bass connects. Saltwater rods and reels are okay with 4/0 or 5/0 hooks.

Sturgeon, rays and other species can also be taken from the bank. Additional county shore fishing areas are Pickleweed Park and Spinnaker Point in the canal area and those places skirting the bay along San Pedro Road such as the Loch Lomond Harbor breakwater and the rockwall before reaching the Brick Yard.

For more information about likely shore fishing locations, call Loch Lomond Live Bait, (415) 456-0321.

Taken at high tide on an overcast day from the bank behind the Pizza Hut, one of many gulls caught in flight. Standing here, you can cast for stripers with success.

PHOENIX LAKE

19

a jewel for all seasons

O F MARIN'S MANY GARDEN spots, Phoenix Lake ranks among the loveliest. Whether wearing fall colors, spring wildflowers, the dusty tan of summer or the cold bareness of winter, this lake's beauty is unsurpassed. Hikers, joggers, horseback riders, bicyclists, nature lovers and fishermen have long found it a convenient and uplifting spot.

To get there, turn off Sir Francis Drake Boulevard in Ross and follow Lagunitas Avenue to the end.

After the torrential rains of February 1985 and a subsequent devastating mud slide that covered the parking area, used by lake visitors, at Natalie Greene Park, access to Phoenix was a bit more difficult. All cars had to park by the tennis courts at Lagunitas and Glenwood Avenues. This required a longer hike, hardest on those fishing.

Repairs are now completed and paved parking facilities are available but still woefully inadequate for the devotees of Phoenix. While Lagunitas Avenue struggles to accommodate the overflow, additional "No Parking" signs newly installed by the town of Ross make the situation even more difficult.

The 25-acre lake is part of the Marin Municipal Water District system. No boats or swimming allowed. Watershed lands surrounding Phoenix are open to daytime use, with many well-kept trails.

The original dirt dam at Phoenix Lake was constructed in 1905 with improvements since. A new spillway, completed in 1986, assures the safety of this facility for years to come.

When the lake was empty for spillway repairs, Marin Conservation Corps with volunteer help anchored clusters of tires to serve as cover for fish populations and constructed gravel spawning beds. Now, with the lake full and clear, young Florida strain largemouth black bass and DFG-planted trout are using the tire clusters for protection.

Steps lead down to the water's edge at both ends of the dam. To the left, there's a fine trail with benches from which to fish and enjoy the magnificent scenery. Or simply rest and bask in the beauty.

Marin Rod and Gun Club's Fish Restoration Committee, in cooperation with MMWD, is striving to make Phoenix Lake a thriving, self-sustaining largemouth black bass fishery, one of the best anywhere. It already is one of the most beautiful.

Down the stairs on the right of the dam and around the path at the water's edge, taken in the cool of the morning on a clear summer day.

FAIRFAX CITY PARK

perfect playground & popular pavilion

W HEN IT COMES to tidy compact recreation areas for outdoor lovers, Fairfax City Park is hard to beat. Though small,
it takes a while to see it all and you'll probably come away
surprised at what's really there.

You might start by parking in front of the redwood grove on
Bolinas Road just before Park Road. A few steps puts you in the beauty of the park with its benches, paths and little bridges. Behind town
hall is the parking area for police and city vehicles. Beneath the trees
it's cool, quiet and impressive, a fine place for rest or solitude.

Should you choose instead to walk south toward Park Road along
Bolinas Road, you'll come to the town hall and police department
entrances. Be sure to study the nearby plaque.

"In appreciation," it reads, "of the efforts of those public spirited
citizens who under the leadership of Andrew A. Devoto, made this
park possible. Dedicated May 14, 1959."

Amble up Park Road past the fire house and youth center. Here is
another plaque, this one in a playground dedicated to Andrew Peri
who was the town's chief of police from 1931–'55. And what a complete and wonderful playground it is with swings, slides and other
well-designed structures challenging the imagination and adventure-
some spirit of youngsters. This area is usually alive and resounding
with excited young voices.

Just beyond is a fine redwood grove with picnic tables and horse-shoe pits beside Fairfax Creek which bisects the park. The Fairfax Women's Club is at the corner of School Street and Park Road with tennis courts nearby. A path crosses a small bridge and climbs the hill to a well-kept baseball diamond.

At the crest of the rise behind the field sits the pavilion, a large old building used for all types of recreation — socials, basketball, games, and so forth. The town rents this hall for appropriate occasions. Call (415) 453-1585 for details.

Meanwhile, enjoy the diversity of Fairfax City Park.

Tall redwoods shelter picnic tables. Wonderful Andrew Peri playground is off to right. Not far ahead, Fairfax Creek trickles by and forms a small pool.

DEER PARK PICNIC AREA
ancient trees, space to roam

21

I F YOU'VE NEVER been to Deer Park picnic area one-half mile west of Fairfax, you're missing a great outdoor experience. This county-maintained facility is worth visiting.

To get there, head out on Bolinas Road and just before reaching famed Deer Park Villa where the grade begins, bear left on Porteous Avenue. Watch for a sign. Follow the narrow pavement to the end and there you are.

Parking is limited but each space is paved and well marked. Walking on broad paths beneath the shade of grand old trees is a distinct pleasure. The canyon is on a heavily-wooded 54-acre parcel with trails leading to Marin Municipal Water District lands beyond.

Dogs must be leashed and overnight camping is prohibited. The very spaciousness beneath the trees may beckon you to relax right there rather than to further explore the canyon. Large old oak, redwood and California laurel trees abound, with sturdy picnic tables, some with grills for barbequing, placed around in a pleasing manner.

Grounds are uncluttered and clean, with restrooms, trash barrels, a drinking fountain and a rustic bridge linking the two picnic areas. The creek is usually dry during the summer.

Just beyond the park is a complex of brightly painted buildings which was once Deer Park School but is now Fairfax-San Anselmo

Children's Center. Colorful artwork by renowned artist, Sashio Yamashito, is in evidence on the buildings.

The infant-toddler program, as required by state law, is enclosed by a chain-link fence. However, the rest of the school site — including playgrounds, fields, volleyball areas, etc. — is available for use by visitors, according to Stanley Seiderman, Associate Director of the Center. "All we ask is for the public to be respectful of the activities of the children and staff of the center."

Deer Park, itself, is old, rustic, enchanting — a good place for rest and relaxation. Or, if you're more adventurous, a trailhead for exploring adjacent watershed lands.

Large groups can use the facilities by permit. For more information call (415) 499-6387.

Early morning sunlight filters through the oaks and laurels of the upper picnic area. Across the road, over a bridge in the redwoods is an additional area with tables and barbeques.

BON TEMPE

22

handicap ramp, gentle trails

MARIN MUNICIPAL WATER District's Bon Tempe Lake serves in many ways. Primary purpose, of course, is to continuously furnish clean fresh water for your home.

The dam was completed in 1948, and attracts nature lovers, birders, bikers, hikers, joggers and anglers. A certain fascination about this 144-acre water supply keeps folks coming back. Good trails surround the lake and if it's changing scenery you're after, here it is!

Those appreciating dense forests with a variety of trees and plants usually prefer the south shore trail which offers, on the whole, good in-the-shade walking.

The north shore trail is more open, climbing occasionally among scattered oaks. Tawny hills dip to the water's edge where, mornings and evenings, deer will be feeding. The view toward Mount Tamalpais and the watershed is spectacular.

Should you not wish to circle the entire lake, about a three-mile hike, have someone drop you at the dam, then drive to the east end by the handicap ramp — the only such facility at any Marin Water District lake — to await your arrival on the north shore trail. If you prefer the forested south side route, you can be picked up when you arrive at Lagunitas Lake parking lot. Or you may choose either of these routes in reverse and be met at the dam.

During spring and fall months, anglers try their luck all around the lake. One of my favorite spots, just over the hill on the north side trail from the parking lot near the dam, has been dubbed Hamburger Cove by local fishermen. Another popular area is across the dam next to the pipe where water is pumped into Bon Tempe from Alpine Lake. Surviving trout have a tendency to congregate here in summer because of colder water and more oxygen.

The Department of Fish and Game stocks Bon Tempe with trout from mid-October to mid-June. There are also largemouth black bass in the lake.

For more information concerning Marin's watershed lands, call Sky Oaks Ranger Station at (415) 459-0888.

Taken from the end of the dam nearest parking area, a corner of Bon Tempe, early on a July morning. At the other end of the dam, where water is pumped in from Alpine, fishing is productive later in the season.

MAGNIFICENT MADRONE

23

short climb, triumphant tree

R IGHT HERE IN Marin is a magnificent madrone tree that every nature lover should see. Many experts believe it to be the largest of its kind anywhere. One thing is certain, once seen such a tree cannot be forgotten.

In the early 1980s, Ruth Markt, widow of a Marin Municipal Water District ranger, lead a group of about 30 up a back trail to show us what she termed "The Tree of Life."

I remember standing there in awe, the group entirely silent, by the massive trunk of a tree obviously the oldest living thing any of us had ever seen, except perhaps a huge redwood.

A year or two later photographer Wilson Galloway and I returned to photograph that tree. Not an ounce of my admiration and appreciation had diminished.

Now there's an easier way to reach the spot.

Start at Lagunitas Lake parking lot below the dam. Bear left past the resident ranger's home. Once up the stairs, a level, lovely, impressive road skirts the lake, winding beneath firs, non-native coulter pines (now being removed for disease control), bay and madrones.

At the head of the lake, stay left. A bit farther take the marked trail up the steep hill toward Pilot Knob. It's about a quarter mile from the Tree of Life.

Words won't come fast once you arrive. You'll be slightly winded and totally awed. Savor the magnificence. Touch the trunk where the bark has peeled off leaving a smooth patina. Walk around it. Calculate how many people holding hands would be needed to match the circumference which is nothing less than astounding, comprised as it is of six main trunks which seem to defy nature's original intent. This is no average tree.

Sadly, the tree's limited foliage indicates its mortality. In terms of slow dying madrones, there isn't much time left. But while The Tree of Life still stands, you owe yourself the overwhelming view of this truly wondrous specimen.

To leave, continue on the trail that brought you in. Soon you'll reach a dirt road. Take it to the right. Steep and dark, it will lead you right down to the parking lot.

Huge madrone, called "Monkey Tree" by visiting children who love to sit in the sheltering arms. Dick, standing to right, dwarfed by the reaching branches, is a six-footer.

LAGUNITAS LAKE

24

enchanted coves, emerald water

MARIN MUNICIPAL WATER District has seven lakes. Lagunitas — an L-shaped little jewel surrounded by redwood, Douglas fir, madrone, bay, live oak, and buckeye trees plus a profusion of wildflowers that change with the seasons — is often regarded as the most beautiful.

One of the best times to visit Lagunitas is when the sun comes out after a heavy rain. The woods will then be dripping and alive, delicately scented from the recent deluge, the forest floor spongy, emerald green with ferns and moss, the road puddled and sometimes slushy. Those feeder streams you cross on the little bridges will perform at their liveliest, cascading happily with a welcome rush of fresh water.

Oldest and smallest of the lakes, its 50-foot high dam was built in 1873, and impounds 23 acres. A favorite of hikers, joggers, nature lovers, horseback riders, bicyclists and fishermen, this is a truly fascinating place.

To reach Lagunitas, take Bolinas Road out of Fairfax, bear left at the wooden sign pointing to Lake Lagunitas. At Sky Oaks Ranger Station stop to pay your $3 per vehicle entry fee. A mile beyond, after skirting the east end of Bon Tempe, is a large paved parking lot. In the nearby redwood grove, at the base of the dam, is a delightful picnic area with a number of sturdy tables and benches.

For your walk around the lake, start here where the hooded spillway from the lake, in winter and spring, funnels overflow torrents into a large pool, forming a lively stream that pours into Bon Tempe lake. The trail is steep beside the flume. Watch your footing. There are stairs to assist in your climb to the dam.

Once there, scan the lake and its enchanted coves, the heavily-wooded hills beyond. Take off in the direction of your choice.

As you circle the lake, remember that, early in 1988, the DFG planted 9,000 rainbow trout, a select Shasta strain of winter spawning fish. An aerator was installed for temperature and oxygen control to help sustain a self-perpetuating fishery.

Whether you fish or enjoy the lake in a different manner, it should be a source of pride to know how unique and special this fishery promises to become. Lovely Lagunitas gets better all the time.

Lagunitas from the road on the left side of the dam. Spit is where the DFG truck plants fish, as shown in the cover photograph by Clif Rattenbury, taken in late March 1988, the day the first half of 9000 special Shasta strain trout were released into their new aerated home.

ALPINE LAKE &
CATARACT TRAIL

25

tumbling freshet, veteran dam

I F YOU'VE NEVER walked even a short way up Cataract Trail near Alpine Dam, there's an adventure in store for you.

Spring is the best time here when wildflowers are bursting forth and the woods are fragrant from rains. Watch your footing; the path can be slippery. Expect a few windfalls and uprooted trees to clamber around. The impressive forest contains a marvelous mix of redwoods, bay, oak and broadleaf maples. Verdant lush ferns and mosses will amaze and delight you.

To get there, take Bolinas Road out of Fairfax for a quarter hour of scenic mountain driving. Continue past the golf course, wind around and down to Alpine Lake, cross the dam and park your car on the left where the road widens at a very sharp curve. The trail begins here. Just a few steps and you're enveloped in peace and solitude, following an arm of Alpine Lake as it narrows to meet Cataract Creek.

From here, the path is a steep one and two-tenths miles to Laurel Dell picnic area with a spectacular series of pools and waterfalls en route. Each pause to rest offers another page in nature's book, something different and exciting to behold.

If you chose not to go the entire route, the walk back to Alpine will seem entirely different. Coming down you'll discover sites you missed going up, making this worthwhile close-to-home mini-adventure all the more fascinating.

Alpine Lake harbors some huge rainbow trout. These elusive fellows are not easy to catch, but worth a try. If you're an angler, the spot where Cataract Creek tumbles into the lake will appeal to you. A nightcrawler three or four feet beneath a bobber might do the trick. Old pros use varying methods with success but, in traditional secrecy of their breed, they're not sharing.

Once back at your car, don't be in a hurry to leave Alpine. That great old dam is over 70 now, and holds a long, narrow 219-acre lake behind it which reaches all the way to the base of Bon Tempe dam. This is a wild and beautiful portion of Mount Tamalpais watershed country, one worth viewing when you can.

From the far side, looking down at the face of the old cement dam, built in 1917, it appears as a steep amphitheater. This architectural achievement of a bygone time is the only cement dam at Marin's water district lakes — the others being dirt. Road across dam, which leads up the mountain, has limited parking at either end.

BOYD PARK

nature in the heart of a city

B OYD PARK IN central San Rafael is an outdoor oasis.

 With 42 acres to roam, some of it steep, most of it wooded with hiking trails ranging from easy to difficult, this is a great place for children, nature lovers, hikers or picnickers and is located, unbelievably, right "downtown" at B Street and Mission Avenue.

First is a great sandy area with swings, rings, slides and ladders for the kids. Blacktopped, rock-bordered paths wind among oaks, firs, eucalyptus, madrone and cypress trees plus an impressive redwood grove. Numerous well-placed picnic tables are available and put to good use, particularly on weekends.

A meandering stream bisects the park in an enchanting manner. Wide planks occasionally bridge the tiny creeklet. Follow a path up the hillside and you're in for a surprise — a goldfish pond of significant proportions fed by a waterfall that splashes, from quite a height, down the face of a blackberry covered cliff. A huge cactus shares the hillside with a tangle of other plants.

Heavy green growth in the pond offers adequate protection and ideal propagating conditions for a splendid population of goldfish ranging from tiny to eight or more inches in length. Cattails and water hyacinths add beauty to the spot.

Cement stairs on either side of the pond reach up the hill, Robert Dollar Drive to the right, steep trails to the left.

When Jayne and I wandered through this park recently we were delighted that such a place exists — a nearby spot to relax and enjoy. She stopped to point out to me the toyon and blooming white ceanothus, also known as wild lilac.

As we returned to the gate house near the park's entrance, we noted that it, with the park, was donated by the Boyd Family to San Rafael in 1905. The elegant old home is now the Marin County Historical Society Museum which is open Wednesday through Sunday from 1 to 4 p.m. For history buffs, a visit here nicely sets the tone for a relaxing sojourn in the park.

Glimpsed through a stand of redwoods, a corner of the sandy sunny playground area. Up the walkway and stairs behind, is pond with large goldfish which delight young visitors.

MCNEAR'S BEACH COUNTY PARK

27

pools, palms & pier

MARIN'S POPULAR McNear's Beach County Park at San Pedro Point now has an added attraction of significant proportions, a $714,000 cement fishing pier reaching 500 feet into San Pablo Bay.

Dedication ceremonies for the sturdy, beautifully designed, safety oriented, T-shaped structure were held June 8, 1988, giving anglers a prime location to try for sturgeon, striped bass and other fish.

McNear's also has 5.5 acres of nicely manicured turf for throwing balls or tossing frisbees, swimming and wading pools, two tennis courts, picnic tables, 70 lovely acres to roam, trails to explore, a mile of rocky beach and a magnificent view of San Pablo Bay.

A sunny winter day is a fine time to visit McNear's Beach. No, the pools won't be open, and perhaps nobody will be playing tennis. The grass may be spongy to your step and all but deserted, and the concession stand will probably be closed, but this affords a degree of solitude that is never there in summer. In winter there's no congestion or overcrowding which at prime times can close the gate to additional pleasure seekers.

Winter, too, is the time of year when sturgeon jump. Walk out to the end of the new pier. Keep an eye peeled to the east and you might just see one of these acrobatic creatures explode from the bay in a way you won't soon forget. When these elusive diamondbacks decide it's time to romp, better have your camera poised. They put on a grand show.

McNear's is clean with tall palms that give the area a tropical touch. The more recent landscaping — wide curving walks and berm-planted shrubs, ground cover and young trees — makes it an altogether attractive space to enjoy various outdoor pleasures. The hills behind are forested with seasoned eucalyptus adequately screening the location from creeping suburbia.

This natural beauty spot is open from 8 a.m. to 8 p.m. May through September. There is a $3.00 per car parking fee; $5.00 on weekends. October through April hours are from 8 a.m. to 5 p.m. weekdays, 8 a.m. to sunset weekends. Fee in winter is $1.00.

Jutting out over water, the new cement pier with the rocky beach exposed by low tide and the Richmond hills across San Pablo Bay. To the right are the snack bar, pools, tennis courts and, up the hill, picnic spots. Load the car with kids and plan to spend a day having fun at this beautiful complete complex.

CHINA CAMP

28

all this — and history, too

RECREATIONAL OPPORTUNITIES abound at China Camp State Park with 1690 acres for nature lovers, hikers, horseback riders, joggers, bicyclists, swimmers, windsurfers, boaters and fishermen, to enjoy. And only minutes from downtown San Rafael!

At Back Ranch Meadows, for instance, there are 30 walk-in campsites (see next article). Day-use picnic areas with tables and running water are found at Buckeye, Weber, China Camp Point and at the village itself.

Ever changing scenery with sudden surprising vistas, greets those who take to any of the many well-maintained trails. Variety is the key to fulfillment at China Camp where meadows, salt marshes, silent forests and magnificent views are all available, a great place for nature studies. You will often see squirrels, deer, an occasional fox and a wide selection of birds. It's easy to escape the stress and shove here, particularly in the oak and laurel forests.

There are even several good spots along North San Pedro road for anglers who like to shore fish. If you're after striped bass, sturgeon, flounder or perch, remember, mud flats extend some distance during low tides. You need water to fish so check your tide book first.

The area is rich in history. In the village is a fascinating, well-maintained museum. Visitor hours are 11-5 Saturdays and Sundays. Once inside, the feeling of how it was from the 1870s to the decline of shrimping after 1911, will overcome you. The weathered boards of the building, the old tools and nets, the many photographs, even the unique smell of the place, bring the past to life.

Back then, before the outlawing of Chinese bag nets in 1911, China Camp was a flourishing village. Great quantities of shrimp were processed, dried and shipped to the Orient.

If you visit the village on a weekend, be sure to stop by the store. They serve a tasty fresh shrimp cocktail and you can usually buy cooked shrimp to take home, both for a modest price.

There's so much to see and do at China Camp's many facilities, more than one visit is necessary to cover it.

State park rules are strictly enforced throughout the entire area. For additional information call (415) 456-0766.

Taken from the parking area above the village on a misty morning, the old wooden pier and weathered building wrapped in peace. Gentle waves lap the beach which still holds a briny trace of drying shrimp, at least in the imagination.

BACK RANCH MEADOWS

29

into the woods, a rustic escape

THERE'S A GREAT place to camp overnight almost within San Rafael's city limits. In fact, you can stay in near seclusion beneath a canopy of oak, California laurel and madrone trees, with a sturdy camp table, a food locker, running water, barbecue pit, and clean restrooms nearby.

You won't have your car because this is a walk-in campground. However, the family vehicle will be parked safely in a large paved lot only a few hundred yards away.

Where is this bit of Shangri-La? Just within the boundaries of China Camp State Park on North San Pedro Road. Watch for the sign that reads, "Back Ranch Meadows Walk-In Campground." Take the road to the right and circle around for 300 yards to the parking area.

Rustic split-rail fences mark the paths to a pair of campsite complexes. Nos. 1-15 lie in the woods along the bottomlands beside a creek bed, usually dry except during a winter storm. There are signs warning of poison oak, and a big old cement cistern, empty now, up the trail a piece. Each camp is large and semi-private with room for relaxing. Many trails lead through wooded hills to the west, or toward San Pablo Bay to the east.

Campsites 16-30 are on a knoll above the creek bed and every bit as attractive and even more secluded than those in the lower section.

During the summer of 1991, improvement work took place. Hot showers were installed, welcome after a day of hiking. Flush toilets now grace the restrooms, and the camp is now handicap-accessible.

All this upgrading means an increase in rates so call (415) 456-1286 for current charges and hours.

Back Ranch Meadows walk-in campground is unique, a place to escape in the true sense and only a very few miles from home. You might even think you're in another world. I did.

This is a view of upper camp, taken in late spring after a dry winter. The peace and quiet are unbelievable; you can hear the songs of birds and the scrambling crackle of small woodland creatures. Since this is a walk-in camp, no engine noise intrudes.

CIVIC CENTER LAGOON

30

circle the pond, nap in the shade

I F A VARIETY of gentle outdoor activities is what you're looking for, try Civic Center Lagoon.

The spacious area is well designed, with paved pathways, green lawns, benches, picnic tables, trash cans and a latrine among the pines at the south end.

About the only taboos here are swimming, wading or boating and pets must be leashed.

At lunch time during the week, expect an invasion of brown-baggers from Frank Lloyd Wright's impressive Civic Center building across the road.

On hand at various times are joggers, bikers, runners, walkers, nature lovers, birders, fly casters, bluegill anglers, duck feeders and dog walkers. A wide paved pathway circles the lake and covers 3370 feet if you walk the entire distance.

Groves of pine trees and weeping willows offer shade on hot days. An island of about one acre, at the north end, serves as a water-fowl sanctuary. Mallards predominate but I saw a variety of other birds including geese, pigeons, blackbirds, and the ubiquitous seagulls.

One young fellow sat on a bench facing the lagoon and island. He had a large bag of bird feed and the feathered population knew it. Hundreds of ducks flocked at his feet as he tossed handfuls to the hungry, squawking masses.

Youngsters can catch small bluegill here using worms beneath a bobber. This is a great place to practice fly casting. Each year the North Bay chapter of Trout Unlimited holds a fly-casting seminar here, with fly-tying demonstrations. This organization encourages catch and release, and all environmentally sound conservation and restoration practices.

When circling Civic Center Lagoon and looking north, the impressive Marin Center complex, where many productions and activities are staged, is visible. The popular Farmers' Market is held in the parking lot here on Thursday and Sunday mornings.

Yes, the lagoon is a fine spot to relax, nap in the grass and feed some ducks.

Only a fraction of the bird life stood still for their photograph! Benches and tables visible under the weeping willows and the lawn stretching down to the water's edge. To the right, out of the picture, is a non-functional series of pools, fountains and waterfalls, the victim of too many dry winters in a row.

MC INNIS PARK

31

wide-open turf, field sports & more

I F YOU WANT space, think John F. McInnis Park.

Newest of Marin's county parks, this 441-acre predominately flat site offers room for hiking, jogging, bicycling, canoeing, fishing or playing soccer, softball and tennis. There are two soccer fields, two Little League size softball stadiums, four tennis courts, players change-house facilities, a canoe launching dock and a model car racing track.

Located at the end of Smith Ranch Road, the park is only a mile from HWY 101's Lucas Valley interchange north of San Rafael. The attractive trellised overhead gateway is just beyond the now rusting rails of the old Northwestern Pacific Railroad. Signs direct you to various locations within the park.

No question, you can find solitude and beauty here with lots to interest outdoor folks. To the west are Marin's wooded slopes. Looking eastward, San Pablo Bay opens at the foot of the tule-fringed slough.

A few openings in the tules allow shore anglers to fish for stripers, flounder or whatever, but this is not the main interest at McInnis. Field sports get the nod and, with a few tables placed strategically, it is a great place for picnicking.

I visited the park on a recent blustery, overcast day and walked acres of playing field turf, enjoying its expanse and the spectacular views of north bay landscapes. You can even see Mount Tamalpais off to the west. Few folks were about. It was a pleasure to inspect the perimeter of the large complex, to know there is a good place close by to escape the freeway hubbub.

Even golfers are not neglected at McInnis. Within the park boundary toward the bay, is a privately operated driving range, a great place to practice your longest shots.

Generally speaking, this vast recreational facility is open during daylight hours.

Leaving the park, I fantasized being stopped by operating railroad gates that indicated an approaching train. And what a boon to Marin commuters were it a nice long string of passenger coaches to help relieve HWY 101's congestion... !

Looking east across the fields with the entrance off to your left. There is a wonderful spaciousness about this park and the paths that wander around it.

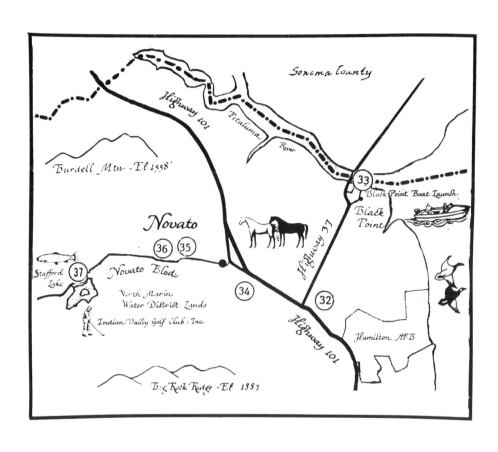

NORTH MARIN

PACHECO POND

catfish, bluegill, crappie — but are there bass?

EVER VISIT Pacheco Pond? Worth investigating, it lies to the right of the two-lane road linking the Bel Marin industrial complex with the Keys proper. There's a large gravelled parking area and a nearby island facing the shore. The place is unimproved, just a few huge rocks placed around which makes it even more intriguing for outdoor lovers.

This wild bit of tule-fringed water is a welcome break in an otherwise urban and suburbanized location. Picnicking is possible on a small flat beneath some veteran eucalyptus trees back from the water's edge.

I checked it out on a blustery Saturday afternoon over one Labor Day weekend. The parking lot held only a half dozen cars and there were perhaps a dozen shore anglers, some of them youngsters. The brackish water was choppy.

"Any luck?" I asked a fellow fishing with his girl.

"One small bluegill," he said. "I threw it back."

"We catch catfish here," volunteered a boy about 11 who was with a couple of companions. "We're just starting."

Another half dozen young anglers were fishing into the wind farther west off a steep bank. As I approached, a fellow held up a fine stringer of crappie and a single catfish. "Got 'em on white Jigs," he said. "Now I'm trying worms."

I'd heard that Pacheco Pond held some striped bass and that the DFG had once planted trout here, since it is a fresh water basin. Only rumors, however.

I remember asking bass fishing pro John Abele, who lives at Bel Marin Keys, about this.

"Well," he said with the slight evasiveness peculiar to fishermen who are guarding a special secret, "there are a few largemouth black bass there. Like to see them take hold better."

Pacheco Pond is not large, but it is a place to escape in a rough sort of way with room enough for biking, walking, road-side jogging, bird-watching, relaxing and, of course, fishing. I'm curious about those elusive stripers and black bass. Looks like a good place for them. Think I'll give it a try.

Steep bank down to the water. Little island upon which three of four planted pines survive, out of picture off to right. Fed by springs and Novato Creek, water here is slightly brackish and the fish population uncertain but worth a try.

BLACK POINT FISHING ACCESS

——————————————————— 33

under the overpass, a ramp with floating piers

ARE YOU AWARE that when you cross Petaluma River on the curved hump of HWY 37 bridge that you're passing over a fine public fishing access and boat launching facility?

To appreciate what's there, follow signs from either direction to Black Point and head toward the river. Here you'll find a compact layout, an ideal spot for boaters and anglers, even picnickers.

Black Point Public Fishing Access on the Marin side of Petaluma River was developed by the Wildlife Conservation Board in conjunction with the California Department of Fish and Game and is operated by County of Marin.

Even though a well-designed facility, it often becomes overcrowded on weekends during the summer and when good angling tides draw boat launchers. A two-lane paved ramp dips into the river at a sensible angle. Nearby to the south are two picnic tables amidst some protective shrubbery, a drinking fountain and trash cans with latrines to the west.

A paved parking area in the shadows of the bridge holds about a dozen cars with boat trailers. Be careful not to park blocking access to a private dock at the north end. When the lot is full there's still room along the road for shoulder parking and across the way to the west is a paved overflow parking area with an additional 18 marked spaces for cars and trailers.

I visited the ramp on a recent Sunday. Because striped bass and sturgeon fishing was hot the place was crowded. Boats were being launched and pulled out with precision and a minimum of delay. There was a general spirit of cooperation and sportsmanship. Pickups and cars towing boats came and went in orderly fashion. This has to be one of the finest free launching facilities in Marin County.

Across the river lies Port Sonoma marina, harbor and bait shop, another place worth visiting. Indeed the mouth of Petaluma River offers unique opportunities in a compact area.

Two fishermen at the end of a float try their luck. Port Sonoma Marina across the river, HWY 37 bridge overhead. This free boat launching ramp is popular when fish are running.

SCOTTSDALE POND

sanctuary saved in sight of freeway

34

I N THE SHADOW of HWY 101 just west of Rowland Boulevard overpass lies Scottsdale Pond, a tule-ringed natural 4-5 acre fresh water lagoon. Chances are, speeding by, you have never noticed.

A few years ago, the City of Novato, with the vote of the people, decided it was worth preserving.

From the viewpoint of those outdoors folks who know the intriguing spot, the $2.5 million required to save Scottsdale Pond was money well spent. A precious piece of Marin's heritage is now firmly preserved for future generations.

"Hard to believe," said retired *Marin Independent Journal* reporter Terry Newell, who lives nearby, "that such a place exists so close to a freeway."

A lot of credit belongs to those responsible for preserving this sensitive natural habitat and a resting area for many species of migrating birds using the Pacific Flyway. It stands as a splendid example of environmental conservation, as is abundantly evident if you simply stop by to watch, feed or photograph the wildlife. There's not a better time than mid-winter. On a recent visit I saw every breed of duck from mudhens to mallards. I also counted geese, swans and, of course, a seagull or two! There are some good places for bird-feeding and watching. All were occupied the Saturday I stopped by.

Once here, freeway noise fades in favor of the fascination of all that's at hand.

Remote-controlled model boats are allowed on the pond from July 1 thru January 31 as long as fuel isn't spilled and speedy operating models stay near the west shore so not to interfere with wildlife habitat.

To arrive at Scottsdale Pond traveling north on 101, take Rowland Boulevard exit, cross over the freeway and make a left on Redwood, the first traffic light. Coming south, exit on Rowland and continue over to Redwood. The pond is on your left with ample parking and plenty of room to picnic, bird watch, fish, walk, run your model boat or simply enjoy...

Cattails along waterline at the the sanctuary where birds float serenely just off shore. Rowland Boulevard overpass shows how close traffic and civilization is.

PIONEER PARK

35

acres graced by history & beauty

P IONEER MEMORIAL Park in North Marin is worth visiting any-time of year — 11.5 lovely acres of historical significance, owned and maintained by the City of Novato.

The intriguing plot faces Novato Boulevard to the south, Simmons Lane to the east while Novato Creek borders the property north and west.

A pioneer family cemetery occupies 3.5 acres of hilltop, some gravesites with headstones dating back to the mid-1800s. Tombstones vary from quite elaborate to simple. Signs of two early attacks by van-dals are still evident despite heroic efforts to restore gravesites to their original condition.

I toured the park recently with retired *IJ* reporter Terry Newell. He did his share years ago to help make this haven a reality.

"Following the cemetery vandalisms," Terry said, "I found out the eight adjacent acres were available. I wrote articles, took the mayor and each councilman to visit, urging them to support obtaining the property and constructing a park."

Newell is modest concerning his role but is proud the way it all turned out. "No vandalism since the city took over," he said.

A row of tall stately old pines, lawns, a fine playground for youngsters and wide curved walkways grace the park. Picnic tables are spread around, particularly beneath the oaks along Novato Creek.

Other attractions include a gazebo and tennis courts, with trails leading here and there.

However, somebody's dream is not in use — a terraced fountain, now dry. Perhaps its many pools are too difficult to maintain and keep functional. Or it may be empty in response to the need for water conservation.

Even so, it's more of a sculpture than a distraction. Throughout, Pioneer Park is a clean, well-planned place to picnic, relax, explore, walk or step back into the past by a leisurely stroll through a pioneer cemetery that is no longer vandalized, thanks to Terry Newell and the City of Novato.

From the pathway in front of old cemetery, looking at the gazebo, rolling lawns spread like a green carpet. Innovative and imaginative playground is up slope at the left.

MIWOK PARK

36

museum, barbeque & a creek with trout

E VER BEEN TO Miwok Park in Novato?
If not, ask those who have. Chances are they'll give you a glowing report.

To get there, head west on Novato Boulevard. Just beyond Eucalyptus Avenue, cross the creek. Be prepared for a sharp right into the paved parking area.

Spacious, well-groomed lawns will greet you, along with a feeling of relaxation mixed with a desire to see more.

The Marin Museum of the America Indian is located here in an attractive two-story building which houses a gallery and gift shop. Hours are from 10–4 Tuesday-Saturday, Sunday 12–4.

My wife, Jayne, and I visited Miwok Park recently and walked the paved pathways as well as some more adventurous trails along the creek and beneath a forest of California laurel, buckeye and massive oak.

We saw an expansive barbeque area with an abundance of well-shaded tables. Nearby were sturdy wooden and pipe play structures, a slide and swings. Across the path were horseshoe pits.

At the west boundary, we found a sign that read, "Novato Rotary Fishing Hole. Constructed as a labor of love, 1986–'87."

Five kids were fishing. One 13-year-old, of Novato, showed us a limit of trout he caught using bread for bait!

While meandering back to our camper we happened upon genial Bob Weil, civil engineer, and a couple of other employees.

"Yes," Bob said, "it's about an 11-acre park, well laid out and maintained by the City of Novato."

We liked the shade, benches, paths, restrooms, the unhurried feeling of being in an atmosphere that underscores outdoor recreation, picnicking and barbequeing.

Park hours are from 8 a.m. to 10 p.m. daily, no motorized vehicles allowed. No horses either, and dogs must be leashed.

However, these few restrictions are designed to enhance enjoyment. Miwok Park certainly qualifies as one of North Marin's best. For fun and relaxation, why not check it out?

Under oaks and bay, one of the sturdy wood structures to challenge youngsters. Some of the picnic tables shown. To the right is Novato Creek, stocked by DFG for those 18 and under.

STAFFORD LAKE

beauty, bass & family fun

37

N OVATO'S STAFFORD LAKE County Park offers variety to families in search of outdoor fun and relaxation.

Acres of well-kept green lawns spread to the water's edge. Various shade trees, including weeping willow and a splendid grove of stately old pines, dot the landscape, with picnic tables and barbeque pits in evidence everywhere. There are some fenced enclosures to shelter large groups.

No question, Stafford Lake is well-maintained with two large parking areas and clean restrooms. One family with little ones was having a great time successfully flying a pair of colorful kites. The wind was just right for it. Nothing like the sound of gleeful laughter.

To add to the fun, a children's playground was completed in the fall of 1988.

East of one parking lot there is a foot bridge and jetty for young anglers. On the day we visited, only a few were fishing the then slightly murky waters. There's a fine view of the lake's only island from here. During spring, surrounding hills are cloaked in green with bright splashes of blooming wildflowers, tanning, of course, by summer.

In 1984, Marin County Parks, North Marin Water District and the Department of Fish and Game, teamed up to help develop a quality warm water fishery at Stafford. The lake was drained, trash fish removed. Old trees and structures were installed to provide habitat and protection for future fish. When refilled the following year, Florida strain largemouth black bass and red-ear sunfish were stocked.

In the next couple of years not many black bass were taken by anglers. DFG conducted a fish population survey after which modifications were made. In 1987, when the lake was low, oak limbs were anchored on the bottom to provide more cover and better habitat. After this, additional plantings were made. Catches are improving and hopes of a self-sustaining fishery are bright.

State fishing license is required for those 16 and older. Limit is five bass per day 12 inches or over. Live bait is prohibited, catch and release encouraged.

As this is North Marin's water supply, no swimming, boats, rafts or waders allowed, but there's enough else to do here for a great family outing. A $3 per car parking fee is required summer weekends. The rest of the time, it's $1.00.

Geese stroll on the spreading lawns. Pine trees and well-placed picnic facilities make this an attractive spot for family outings.

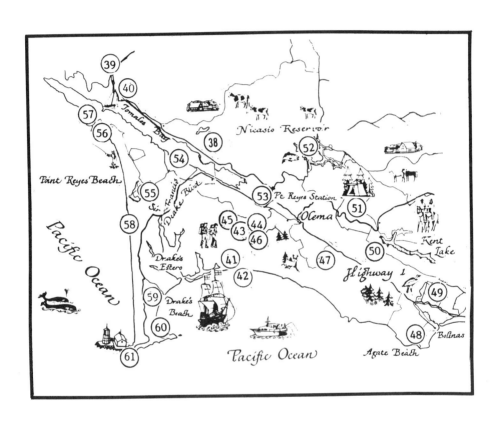

WEST MARIN

SOULAJULE LAKE

38

remote & worth the trek

MARIN MUNICIPAL WATER District's mystery lake is its youngest, Soulajule, finished in 1979, 106 years after the oldest, Lagunitas. Ever been there? If so, you're probably one of our more adventurous outdoor people.

Not the easiest place to find, it's impressive when you do, particularly if you're a hiker, angler or in love with Marin's varied and ever-changing terrain.

I first visited Soulajule several years ago with my fishing buddies, Mike Mirko of San Anselmo and Wilson Galloway, Richmond. We liked the hills, the remote feeling, the magnificent scenery.

Since it was a weekday, there were few other anglers. The lake is large with many coves, and harbors good populations of bluegill and largemouth black bass with an occasional trout.

We didn't know what we were doing, used worms on bobbers, caught small bluegill but no bass. Those in the know don't talk but come away with some impressive largemouth black bass in the 2-3 pound range and larger.

Things have improved a bit since then. Now there's a sign as you enter the area that reads, "Soulajule Reservoir, one mile. No swimming, firearms, dogs or boats - open sunrise to sunset."

I revisited Soulajule recently on a weekend and found little change. Still remote, exciting, different. Water was murky, fishing fair, the outgoing flow to Walker Creek restricted. The west shore near the dam where a caretaker's home sits is MMWD property, part of the east shore abuts private land. Areas are marked. No more than a dozen cars were parked below the dam or across over in the private sector. That's the way it usually is.

To get to Soulajule, travel north on the Point Reyes-Petaluma road. One mile beyond Marin's famed Cheese Factory bear left on Hicks Valley (Wilson Hill) road, drive three miles over hilly cow country to Marshall-Petaluma road, bear left for another three miles.

Just before Walker Creek, turn left for Soulajule, stay with the narrow pavement beyond the slide area, bear right across the bridge and park in the gravelled zone beneath the dam. That's where your adventure begins.

Where hills and woods come down to the water, the distinctive log boom spans the lake near the dam and spillway. This is just one corner of the large impoundment.

KEYES CREEK FISHING ACCESS

39

roadside spot for winter runs

W HEN STEELHEAD FISHING breaks wide open after a good winter rain, better consider giving Keyes Creek Public Fishing Access on HWY 1 six miles north of Marshall a try.

Although overgrown and rundown after several years with poor fishing, there's a gravelled parking area here to accommodate about 20 cars. The two sturdy picnic tables were table-top high in grass and wild flowers the last time I visited but the latrine and trash cans were clean and maintained. Access trails still lead to nearby Walker Creek where you'll find adequate casting room. One trail even harbors a bench shaded by bushes.

Despite the lack of rainfall in recent winters, a few steelhead are taken along here each year, both with lures and drifted or stationary baits.

If the sea-going rainbow trout are running during January and February, you might find Keyes Creek crowded on weekends. During the week, there will likely be lots of space.

This facility provides an interesting place to relax, picnic and fish. Should you find it overcrowded, there will still be room to cast from the shoulder of the road a quarter mile south where HWY 1 borders Walker Creek with space for roadside parking.

Keyes Creek Access came into being in 1985, the coordinated effort of Marin Municipal Water District, Marin Conservation Corps, and the Department of Fish and Game with an assist by a Fish and Wildlife enhancement grant under the Davis-Grunsky Act, administered by the Department of Water Resources.

Trout Unlimited, under the direction of Leo Cronin, Fairfax conservationist, is involved in ongoing efforts to improve the Walker Creek environment and creek bed. They continue to have weekend work parties to restore the habitat to accommodate returning steelhead.

From a historical standpoint, there's another fascinating facet to the place. It was along here the old North Pacific Coast narrow gauge railroad used to ply en route to Tomales, Occidental, Duncan Mills and beyond. Nearby are the cement supports to an old railroad bridge that once crossed Walker Creek.

Listen closely and you can probably imagine the haunting cry of a steam engine's whistle echoing down the canyon.

Walker Creek below the confluence with Keyes Creek on the left. Just south of here are the old railroad abutments, and to the north, HWY 1 bridge, above which fishing is prohibited.

MILLER PARK

40

down the ramp & into the bay

I F YOU'RE a small boat owner and like adventure, try launching at Miller Park Public Fishing Access on Tomales Bay at Nick's Cove, four miles north of Marshall on HWY 1.

The six-acre site has a large paved free parking area for cars and trailers, picnic tables, toilets, trash cans, a jetty and a public fishing pier where no license is required. However, shore anglers need one. There's a great view of Tomales Bay, Hog Island, the mouth of Walker Creek and all those hidden little beaches and coves across the way.

This is a great place to catch rubberlip perch or start drift fishing with live bait for halibut when they're running. And it's not too far from the open sea.

The park is operated by Marin County, the launching facility funded by Department of Boating and Waterways. The Wildlife Conservation Board and Department of Fish and Game developed the site.

Open from 5 a.m. to 10 p.m., no overnight camping or fires allowed and pets must be on a leash.

Most folks don't leave here without visiting Ruthie Gibson, proprietor of Nick's Cove, an adjacent rustic seafood restaurant and bar with a salty nautical atmosphere. Patrons flock there on weekends, many for barbequed oysters in the half shell. We traditionally stop by for a dozen. Nick's is closed Mondays and Tuesdays.

This area is rich in history, for it was along here the old North Pacific Coast narrow gauge railroad hugged the eastern shore of Tomales Bay. If the train still ran, the rails would cut directly in front of the restaurant and bisect Miller Park.

At many places between Point Reyes Station and Nick's Cove, you can look down and see cuts, fills and bridge abutments where the old railroad right-of-way ran along the water's edge. It's an exercise in nostalgia to trace the route and use your imagination to perhaps hear, see and smell an old diamond-stacked woodburning locomotive puffing by, pulling a few warped coaches...

Float, boat ramp and breakwater at Miller Park. Directly across Tomales Bay, cresting the ridge by the sparse stand of trees, is Pierce Point Road which ends at trails to Tomales Point and McClure's Beach. Hog Island is just out of sight on the right.

MUDDY HOLLOW
TRAIL HEAD

41

the adventure begins here

I F YOU HAVEN'T been to Muddy Hollow, you'll find it a great starting place for a worthwhile Point Reyes National Seashore experience.

Muddy Hollow, a trailhead with signs that give locations and distances, has ample tree-shaded parking. Put your car in a sheltered spot
and walk in any direction. There are a number of options and one
should fulfill your outdoor expectations for the day. If picnicking is
what you want, there's a venerable cypress grove at old Muddy
Hollow Ranch, just a few yards east, that should please you.

Another good choice is the hike west to Limantour Beach, a two-
mile level walk through fast-changing scenery — alders, willows, coy-
ote brush, lagoons, bald hills and wind-swept beaches.

In the wet season, the trail may be swampy in spots and you'll
probably see some rabbits and ducks en route. If you're an angler, you
may locate trout in the first large pond. I took a few one windy day
where a break in the tules gave me room to cast.

Should you care to take a quarter-mile hike beyond that cypress
grove where you may have picnicked, walk along an old road beneath
trees and beside a hidden streamlet you can hear but seldom see. The
road then skirts a broad field to the right and soon approaches a

breech in an old levee caused by the devastating storm of 1982 which closed Limantour Road for two years. Since, the farm pond behind the broken levee is gone, but it was once a prime rainbow trout location, a secret spot veteran anglers kept to themselves.

All that's left now of this once pristine pond is a willow-clad bowl and the jagged cut in the dam, mute testimony to both the destructiveness and recovery of nature.

To reach Muddy Hollow, take Sir Francis Drake Boulevard through Olema, bear left at the brown Point Reyes National Seashore Headquarters sign, drive for about two miles to the Limantour sign, take another left for the nine-mile drive over the hill. This is fascinating country, West Marin at its best.

Beyond the gate, under a canopy of alder and willow, a sylvan walkway with trails branching off to many places.

LIMANTOUR BEACH

42

surf & sand unlimited

L IMANTOUR BEACH EXEMPLIFIES expanse, freedom and beauty, a veritable wind-swept paradise. There is much to see and enjoy here with refreshing salt-tinged breezes always at hand in various velocities. As a natural area set aside to protect coastal forms of life, the taking of plants and animals is prohibited.

Thankfully, this is part of Point Reyes National Seashore. It almost wasn't. In the 1950s, Limantour Beach and adjacent nearby Muddy Hollow were beset with stakes and fluttering blue and red flags earmarking a great maze of half-acre homesites.

What we have now, thanks to conservationists, the National Park Service and other concerned citizens who intervened to halt the commercial development, is a rich heritage to be enjoyed in perpetuity.

No, you don't see the golf course that was planned, or elegant houses with no trespassing signs, crowning the ridges. Instead, you can drink in a panorama of enchanting charm and beauty, a breathtaking sweep of seascape on a great stretch of sandy beach arcing in both directions.

A paved pathway leads to the beach from a large parking area. As you walk briskly along, notice ponds and marshes on either side, undisturbed nature at its best.

If it's a weekend and spring weather is in full bloom, there will probably be plenty of people about. But if you're at all adventurous, that doesn't have to last long. Once at the beach, walk either south or

106

north. South you can have your pet on a leash. North is wilderness, no pets, and you won't have to go far to be by yourself.

There are many alternatives once you reach Limantour, as trails branch off in all directions, most clearly marked.

The road to Limantour is paved all the way, reconstructed since the devastating storm of January, 1982.

To get there, take Sir Francis Drake Boulevard toward Inverness, bear left at White House Pool, go a mile to a right turn, then nine curving spectacular miles over the hill to Limantour.

Windswept, wild and wide, breakers crash endlessly on miles of sand at Limantour Beach.

BEAR VALLEY
VISITOR CENTER

43

a place to learn, to plan, to enjoy

I F YOU HAVEN'T been to the Bear Valley Visitor Center near Olema, give yourself a treat and go.

The high-peaked classic barn-like building which houses a great store of outdoor information, is an architectural achievement that blends in perfectly with surrounding meadows and forests.

Within the structure are 2500 square feet of impressive and fascinating exhibits extolling the wonders of Point Reyes National Seashore. Everything is done exquisitely. No over-crowding. Signs hang from the ceiling in a pleasing manner, giving pertinent quotes and facts. This is an all-out attempt to tell the Point Reyes story the way it should be told. My friend, Jack Mason, Marin's late and great historian, indeed would be proud.

Even on a cold, blustery, threatening day the expansive parking area is likely to be full. And you may even find picnickers at the tables beneath mossy-trunked firs and wind-bent oaks. It takes more than weather to keep the adventurous away.

Private foundations contributed $1.4 million for the cost of the building, which was completed in late 1983. The structure was designed by Henrik Bull, interior exhibits by Dan Quan.

Most impressive to me, once inside, was the uncluttered feeling and the great enlarged photos which set the proper tone for this area's rich heritage. The center is open 9 a.m. to 5 p.m. weekdays, 8 a.m. to 5 p.m. weekends and holidays.

Featured are the coastal wetlands, forests, grasslands and the open ocean, each underscored and labeled by impressive photos.

In the auditorium I saw a 23-minute movie entitled "Something Special." And that's exactly what it was, adding visual significance to the area.

The superbly designed interior even harbors soft chairs and a wood stove for the comfort of patrons on cold days.

I came away knowing Point Reyes National Seashore is a monumental achievement in foresight and preservation that will always enhance the glory and beauty of this land.

Looking back at the Visitors Center from the trail to Kule Loklo. Behind, the Morgan Horse Ranch.

EARTHQUAKE TRAIL

44

are you ready for the big one?

I F YOU'D LIKE an informative, revealing outdoor adventure, walk the Earthquake Trail near Bear Valley Visitor Center, Olema.

This paved six-tenths of a mile loop is suitable for wheelchairs. Since we live in earthquake country, the visuals on the trek give great insight and you'll come away better prepared to handle a major quake when the next big one strikes.

A self-guiding nature trail, fascinating from the start, the signs along the way keep you informed. In no time you' re passing bearded oaks, California laurels, giant firs, huge blackberry patches and other forms of tangled undergrowth.

Soon you cross a lively, willow-banked creek on a footbridge with handrails, and as the trail bears south, there on the hillside is a series of blue posts. These mark the shift of the San Andreas fault resulting from the great quake of April 18, 1906 which measured 8.3 on the Richter scale.

It was here that Matilda, the cow, supposedly got swallowed by a split in the earth with only her feet and tail showing. Versions of the legend vary, but all agree that Matilda was somehow entombed by the tremor.

This location is but a few miles from where an early morning North Pacific Coast narrow gauge passenger train got dumped on its side by the force of the quake just prior to its time of departure.

At almost any museum in Marin you can see a copy of the famous picture — the overturned train, its engineer, a girl and a dog.

Another impressive example of the force is an old fence that still stands with a 16-foot gap at one point caused by the quake. The fence stops abruptly, then continues on up the hill 16 feet farther south!

It would be hard to leave Earthquake Trail without learning that continents drift because of moving plates, and that moving plates cause earthquakes which also explains why there are two different kinds of rock here — Franciscan and granite.

Quoting from one of the last signs, "We can expect another big quake soon."

Are you prepared?

A view of the fence that slipped 16 feet sideways in the 1906 earthquake.

KULE LOKLO

they used the land gently

K ULE LOKLO, THE Coast Miwok Cultural Exhibit, is an evolving coastal Miwok village near the Bear Valley Visitor Center in Olema. This quarter-mile walk into our past is well worth taking when you're in the area. Work on the authentic exhibit began in 1976 and has taken National Park Service employees and hundreds of volunteers all this time developing the village. The process continues.

There are signs en route to keep you informed. The trail skirts part of Point Reyes Morgan Horse Farm pasture, winds through bearded old oak trees, tall Douglas firs with venerable eucalyptus and cypress in evidence.

Where deer, elk, bear and other animals once roamed, now there are horses. A sign says, "Wildlife Area — no dogs."

As you approach Kule Loklo, the Coast Miwok words for Bear Valley, a fascinating layout appears.

You learn from signs along the way that the Coast Miwoks ate plants, fish and mammals but did not practice agriculture. They left the environment unspoiled while learning to use those resources available to them.

Homes were conical wooden frames covered with redwood bark that lasted for years. Others were made by tules thatched to willow frames or layers of brush piled on a wooden framework.

Acorns were a staple food of the Miwoks supplemented by meats, seeds, fruits and vegetables. These were stored in several types of granaries built along the same lines as their houses except usually of larger dimensions.

Those arbor-like structures acted as sunshades for basketmakers, beaders, flint knappers and a place for acorn processing.

Walking the sloping trail, you can suddenly see an unmarred vista across the valley to the distant hills, apparently unchanged since the Miwoks pursued their quiet lives here.

Kule Loklo is a recreated wonder that certainly gives us a feeling for the Miwoks' daily lives and the simplicity of their culture.

Once they numbered an estimated 3,000: By the 1800s less than 50 pure-blooded Coast Miwoks remained. Now there is this.

A village in the process of becoming, shown is one of the conical redwood bark homes. Built with the materials and in the manner of the Miwoks, slowly a former way of life is emerging for those in the present to learn from.

WOODPECKER TRAIL

a forest for the birds

O F THE MANY trailheads beginning at National Seashore Headquarters, Olema, don't overlook Woodpecker Trail. This self-guiding loop of less than a mile shows the amazing hand-iwork of a multitude of woodpeckers in the trees of their preference. New wayside exhibits have been installed to add to your pleasure and knowledge as you take this walk.

The trail starts with a sign and a gentle climb. Soon you're in deep forest and come upon one of many Douglas firs, giant old trees with heavily perforated bark. It's hard to believe that the myriad of holes were made by woodpeckers, not machine guns.

Despite years of apparent abuse by birds somehow drawn to these particular firs, most trees are still alive and thriving, massive monsters holding on to satisfy the needs of their needling feathered friends.

It was rainy and cold when I walked this trail, adding to a deli-cious solitude. I met no other hikers which somehow increased my reverie. Open spots were green and spongy, the woods dripping and scented as I ducked and dodged gnarled trunks and low branches. Not a woodpecker was visible or audible that day.

Then there was a chuckling stream to my left, hardly visible beneath heavy undergrowth where green ferns nodded gently to the beat of raindrops. Following the map I had studied, I bore to the right here.

Soon I broke out of the forest and was abreast of the Morgan Horse Farm. A sign with an arrow pointed back toward my starting point.

Then, near the parking area, I found myself reading a sign about America's first native breed of horse. These animals are noted for their stamina, dependability and intelligence. There were two or three up pasture from me. They looked sleek and happy in the rain.

General Sherman rode a Morgan named Fancy. Phil Sheridan's was Rienzi, two famous men on two famous horses.

The horses here are trained as ranger patrol mounts while the Douglas firs host woodpeckers. What an interesting day!

One of the wood-peckers' favorite "storage lockers," an old pine tree shows a multitude of holes. No one knows why this batch of trees, above all others in the vicinity, is chosen by the peckers.

FIVE BROOKS TRAILHEAD
47

pack up & head out

FOR EXCITING OUTDOOR opportunities, start at Five Brooks Trailhead just off of Shoreline Highway, three and a half miles south of Olema. Watch for the brown Point Reyes National Seashore sign. Turn right.

Five Brooks is an important key to the vast wilderness areas of Point Reyes National Seashore. Take your time studying the fine map listing intriguing trails with distances to camping places and other remote and historic points of interest.

The trailhead is two-tenths of a mile up a gravelled road just beyond the horse stables. There's a large parking area, latrines, trash cans, a drinking fountain and ample flat land for picnicking with a few tables scattered about. Also, there is a circular horse trough with a plaque to the memory of Sonny Zappetini who was a dedicated horseman. Horses are allowed on many of the park trails and can be rented at Five Brooks Stables, (415) 683-8287, or at Bear Valley Stables, (415) 663-1570.

Nearby is a willow-fringed pond with equestrian trails all around. At the south end, a tall pipe feeds a steady stream of water into the lake creating a captivating splash. During the 1950s, a large sawmill was located here.

Tules and algae clog the surface. The day I visited, a magnificent blue heron stood on a mid-pond stump passively enjoying his domain. Turtles sunning themselves on logs are not uncommon here.

The area is geologically complex. For instance, Pine Gulch and Olema creeks run parallel but drain in opposite directions, an oddity undoubtedly connected with the San Andreas fault. The popular five mile long Rift Zone trail follows the fault north from Five Brooks to Bear Valley. Most trails at Five Brooks begin by circling the duck pond counterclockwise and are clearly marked. Stewart Trail is an old logging road which eventually meets Ridge Trail. There are many others. The Greenpicker Trail is popular with horseback riders.

Camping is by permit only, free at Bear Valley headquarters near Olema. Dogs are prohibited on trails. No firearms, motor vehicles or open fires allowed.

One thing is certain. You have a fine selection. Plan your hike carefully and come prepared.

Through a break in the foliage, the algae-covered pond, ringed with tules, cattails and trees, where many exciting hikes and horseback rides begin.

AGATE BEACH

48

tide pools & history

C HANGING WITH the tides from an extensive pool-potted reef to a narrow strip of pebbly sand, Agate Beach, near Bolinas, is unusual and historic. Visiting here is a memorable outdoor adventure.

Take HWY 1 south out of Olema. Just before reaching the lagoon, bear right on the unmarked road that leads into Bolinas proper. Turn right on Mesa Road, go about a mile to Overlook and make a left, then right on Elm for one and a half miles to the Agate Beach Public Fishing Access on your left. There's a broad paved parking area here protected by bluffs. Signs direct you to the beach.

Nature is at work here all the time. As I walked along the rocky beach, there was a constant clicking sound — pebbles slipping off the face of cliffs. It was low tide, the pools active with marine life. The rough-shod long curving beach, between Bolinas Point and Duxbury Point, is a great place for rock hounds, souvenir hunters, hikers, joggers, birders, anglers and history buffs.

Each year a Sir Francis Drake celebration takes place there with a hundred or so interested folks hiking around reliving the days over 400 years ago when Sir Francis Drake visited the area. The sixth such annual event took place in June 1988, the group led by San Rafael historian George Epperson.

George has what he claims is irrefutable proof that Sir Francis Drake beached the Golden Hinde here for repairs in 1579, and not in

Drake's Estero, as history so often states. At Epperson's home recently, I saw much of his collection and it is convincing. He also has a large abalone shell filled with bullets and a box of fishing sinkers. "Found them all at Agate Beach," he said, "along with many historic artifacts."

Drake's Fort was here below Point Bolinas and not far from where the famed buccaneer's claim plate of brass was found by Jeff Graves over 50 years ago. Entrenchments are still visible.

Regardless, Agate Beach is capable of firing your imagination either historically or with the teeming sea-life in the pools or, if you're like George Epperson, by the bits of history hidden in the pebbly beach. You might even find an agate!

Pathway down to Agate Beach from the access parking lot. Tide is low, the reef and tidepools exposed. During wild winter storms, waves crash between these jutting cliffs and halfway up the path.

AUDUBON CANYON RANCH

49

through a telescope, a peek in the nests

A HAVEN FOR outdoor lovers, Audubon Canyon Ranch, Bolinas Lagoon Preserve, is a privately owned wildlife sanctuary supported by contributions from its many friends.

The ranch is also ideal for picnickers, environmentalists, conservationists and hikers. Spring and early summer are great times to visit because of nesting herons and egrets, visible in the treetops in a stand of splendid old redwoods known as the Schwartz Grove Rookery.

The early May day my wife and I visited was a good choice. We were met by general manager Maurice "Skip" Schwartz who took us on a personal tour that proved both educational and inspirational. He escorted us through the bookstore and display hall while explaining their various projects and vigorous docent training program.

We then met a visiting Sacramento couple, were loaned telescopes and followed them up the trail to the overlook, a 20 minute walk. They were experienced birders and helped us zero in on numerous nesting egrets and blue herons in the treetops below. And what a great view of the birds' feeding grounds at Bolinas Lagoon in the distance.

This is a paradise for hikers. There are eight miles of trails, some steep, all challenging and exciting. Signs guide the way, give distances and otherwise keep you informed. The two easiest loops are to the overlook and the Harwell nature trail. Others are longer and more difficult with their own fascination.

Garden Club and Picher canyons run parallel with trails circling both.

Audubon Canyon is a worthwhile experience. Docents are well-informed and eager to answer your questions. The grounds are neat, buildings clean. Don't let a visit here escape you...

The ranch is open to the public weekends March through mid-July, 10 a.m. to 4 p.m. Weekdays are reserved for schools and other groups, Tuesdays through Fridays by appointment. For further information call (415) 868-9244.

From the overlook without a telescope, the nesting birds appear as scraps of tissue paper in the tree tops! Beyond is Bolinas Lagoon where they feed — the other half of the combination that brings the beautiful egrets and mighty herons here.

KENT LAKE

50

wild, beautiful & hard to reach

I F YOU' RE A vigorous outdoor person and love scenic beauty, don't overlook Kent Lake. There's no easy access, but you'll be delighted when you see it.

About one mile west of the village of Lagunitas on Sir Francis Drake Boulevard, cross a green-railed bridge. Beneath flows Lagunitas (also called Papermill) Creek just before its confluence with San Geronimo Creek. No room for parking here.

However, about 300 yards down the road beyond the Samuel Taylor State Park sign, there's room on the right for perhaps a half dozen cars at best. Since this is quite a trek, a light pack and a picnic lunch is advisable plus a fishing rod if you're an angler.

Hike back to the bridge, take the left Marin Municipal Water District road up Lagunitas Creek towards Peters Dam. It's nearly a half mile walk to Kent Lake, the last part quite steep.

Once you crest Peters Dam, be prepared for an unexpected view of steep, heavily forested slopes reaching right to the water's edge. The lake is long and slim with many coves — rugged country for the most part with few trails. Even on weekends you won't have to go far here for solitude.

Peters Dam was first built in 1953 and enlarged in 1981 in anticipation of Marin's future water needs. The scarred hillside to the west is a result of excavating for this enlargement.

There's something awesome and magnificent about the view. From the skyline to the lake is wild, beautiful country, an indelible scene your mind can't erase.

As for the fishing, this lake has trophy rainbow trout to five pounds and larger, plus good populations of largemouth black bass and bluegill. However, it's tough to locate, or reach, productive spots. Veteran anglers in the know do succeed but they aren't talking.

Blues are easiest to catch and can be taken from the dam using light gear, worms and bobbers. Hard to reach coves often produce bluegill and largemouth bass with an occasional trophy trout. The trek is worth it, if only for the surroundings — quiet unsurpassed beauty.

Winding miles up the canyon between wooded hills, Kent is long and narrow. Taken from the right side of dam, standing above the steep banks that cut down to the water's edge.

SAMUEL P. TAYLOR STATE PARK

51

picnic or camp — splendor in the woods

SAMUEL P. TAYLOR State Park is always an interesting place to visit no matter how many times you may have been there.

The spacious 2600 acres offer a variety of sharp topographical contrasts to intrigue the outdoor lover. Each season is special. In spring, the area becomes a wildflower enthusiast's dream with numerous varieties adding color to the fascinating region.

Canyons are cool, fern-filled and shaded by coastal redwoods, madrone, Douglas fir and laurel. There are open grassland areas and bald hills, a fine network of trails and fire roads, ideal for hiking and excellent for nature studies.

Bicyclers are not neglected here. A paved trail runs about three miles from near the park entrance to Tocaloma. Scenic, almost level with no vehicular traffic, it's ideal for family bike rides. Actually you' re following the old North Pacific Coast railroad right-of-way.

As for camping, there are 68 sites with tables, woodstoves, food lockers and parking space. If all are occupied, which is generally the case weekends during the summer, don't overlook the group camp areas. There are two of them at Madrone, 300 yards west of the park entrance. For advance reservations call district headquarters at (415) 456-5218.

Then there's Devil's Gulch with a camp for horsemen, and others with corral, water troughs, hitching racks and a capacity of 25 people. The main picnic area is in a redwood grove near Lagunitas (Papermill) creek with tables and stoves.

The entire area is rich in history. In the 1850s Samuel P. Taylor bought 100 acres in the park which now bears his name and built a paper mill. A small town of perhaps 100 families formed around the mill. When the railroad came through in 1874, a hotel was built and Camp Taylor opened. Then, as now, it was a popular recreation area.

The stream was once full of silver salmon and steelhead. Now it is closed to fishing in an attempt to rehabilitate fish populations. However, recreation opportunities abound even without fishing. Plan to picnic there, or make reservations to camp in the redwood's glory.

Entrance to Samuel P. Taylor Park, picnic area to the left and campgrounds reaching into the woods ahead.

NICASIO LAKE

52

open space, windswept water

W HAT DO YOU DO at Marin's largest lake if you can't go boating, swimming or even wading?

Lots. There's hiking, bird watching and fishing for channel catfish, largemouth black bass, crappie, bluegill and huge carp.

I'm talking about Lake Nicasio in West Marin.

Most of you have probably seen the way the lake sneaks in and out of coves, disappears, reappears and makes you wonder just where it does go and why.

Marin Municipal Water District's largest reservoir occupies 889 surface acres with 22.5 miles of shoreline along which 4.35 miles have been developed with turnouts for parking, trash barrels and some latrines.

One finger of the lake begins behind the town of Nicasio's historic red schoolhouse. There's parking and bank fishing here, a pleasant spot that can produce catfish, bluegill or bass.

Due to prevailing winds and large carp cruising the coves and stirring up mud in the shallows, the lake is murky for the most part, but only downright muddy following severe storms.

Built in 1982, Nicasio has changed little since it first filled, except for the 1976–'77 drought when it was so empty the narrow old roads were exposed. Even in years of normal rainfall, the water level fluctuates somewhat through evaporation and pumping.

This is intriguing country — rolling hills, wind-sheared trees, rugged ravines, outcroppings of rocks. The wide expanse of Nicasio and the numerous coves, makes it easy to totally escape civilization with a blanket and picnic basket. A brisk 20 minute walk away from the road at several locations will give you an adventurous feeling. Some parts of the lake are so remote you aren't likely to see another soul.

The fishing, though seldom really hot, is always challenging. Some big channel catfish have been taken and the same with largemouth bass. It would be a better fishery were it not for the nest-foraging carp. Too bad they weren't removed during the drought!

Most anglers, however, are after crappie and bluegill. These fish are taken in coves close to the road using worms beneath a bobber, or with crappie jigs. It's fun, and they're fine eating.

An expanse of Nicasio, thistles and grasses of summer in the foreground. The dam is to the right, the lake and its many coves spreading to the left.

WHITE HOUSE POOL

53

migratory route for fins & feathers

AFTER WINTER RAINS come, Marin residents are happy, and steelhead anglers head for White House Pool between Point Reyes Station and Inverness on Sir Francis Drake Boulevard.

They aren't the only ones: Picnickers, bicyclists, joggers and bird watchers, find this historic spot at the mouth of Lagunitas (also called Papermill) Creek, up to HWY 1 bridge, a great place for outdoor exploration.

Parking is no problem. Stop at the paved public access area just before a sharp bend in Sir Francis Drake Boulevard. Here you'll find adequate space, a latrine and trash cans. Marin County teamed up with the Department of Parks and Recreation, Wildlife Conservation Board, DFG and the State Resources Agency to build this worthwhile facility.

A short walk west along a broad level area above the slough brings you to White House Pool. The trail east leads upstream through grasses, brambles and thickets, a popular area for birders since surrounding wetlands attract many migrators. At least one rare species is spotted annually, bringing in a covey of enthusiasts with binoculars to check out the find.

Benches are spaced at intervals along the levee for the convenience of anglers, picnickers and others. A footbridge crosses Olema Creek just above its junction with Lagunitas.

Upstream a short walk is the site of the controversial Giacomini gravel dam which gets washed out every winter and is bulldozed

128

backed into existence each spring to supply water for dairy cows and irrigation. Many anglers blame the recent sharp decline in steelhead and silver salmon populations on the dam.

Marin history books often make reference to the abundance of steelhead and salmon at White House Pool in West Marin's early days. Whatever the reasons, it's not like that now.

Lagunitas Creek can be fished only up to the HWY 1 bridge a mile to the east but not beyond. A state angling license is required and must be in your possession.

If you haven't visited White House Pool, give it a try if only for rest and relaxation.

Standing on the trail, looking upstream toward HWY 1 bridge. The dark triangle mid-picture on the right is where Olema Creek flows into Lagunitas.

TOMALES BAY STATE PARK

54

camp in the woods, play on the beaches

A GOOD PLACE to go any time of year for outdoor fun is Tomales Bay State Park. You can swim, fish, dig clams, hike, jog, barbeque, picnic, or camp. Or hunt mushrooms. About this, a sign, complete with pictures, warns even experts can be fooled and that some of the world's most poisonous mushrooms, Death Caps and Destroying Angels, grow here.

There are miles of trails leading to four beaches — Indian, Pebble, Heart's Delight and Shell. The road leads to a paved parking area at Heart's Delight Beach with restrooms, picnic tables and barbeque facilities. Hikers never cease to marvel at views of Tomales Bay encountered from various trails. A fascinating place, it is blessed with a weather pattern sunnier, milder and far less windy than along the ocean.

Developers had designs here. However, vigilant and farsighted conservationists were able to purchase 185 acres at Shell Beach in 1945, followed by another 840 acres in 1951. The state then combined the two parcels into a park. A plaque by the Marin Conservation League is dedicated to the memory of Bruce and Ellie Johnstone who helped bring the park into being November 8, 1952.

Picnic tables and barbeque facilities are pleasingly placed beneath mossy bearded oak, laurel and pine trees. Undergrowth is dense with ferns and toyon bushes.

At Heart's Delight Beach instructions are posted for digging Littleneck, Washington and Gaper clams with pictures of each. It's a good place for a swim. No boats or dogs on the beach. The one and a half mile Indian Loop Trail begins here.

To get to Tomales Bay State Park, take Sir Francis Drake highway out of Inverness for two and a half miles to Pierce Point Road on your right. Follow signs to the park entrance.

During off-seasons, the place is not crowded. Entrance fees are posted and you pay by the honor system — put your money in an envelope and drop it in the pipe. For more information call (415) 669-1140.

Fence and trees along the entrance from the parking lot to Heart's Desire Beach on Tomales Bay. Picnic tables to the right, trails through the hills start at both ends of the beach.

ABBOTT'S LAGOON

55

through the pasture & over a stile

E VER BEEN TO Abbott's Lagoon?

This secluded spot on the moors of West Marin is worth visiting. Whatever your outdoor interests, there's something here for you. Not only of historical significance, but being there gives any visitor a feeling of the real West Marin — bald hills, intriguing vistas, salt-tinged winds, an experience of freedom and exuberance.

When Jayne and I visited, the day was only average weatherwise but special because we had with us a picnic basket and a good friend, Barbara Phelps, of Mill Valley.

No trouble finding the place. Take Sir Francis Drake through Inverness, bear right on Pierce Point Road toward Tomales Bay State Park but don't enter there. Continue on Pierce Point for a mile and a half to a small parking lot with toilets. You're only a mile from the Pacific Ocean with an easy, fascinating walk that takes you through a pasture and over a stile. It's quiet except perhaps for the sound of a sea breeze, birds or the distant rumble of the surf. No motor vehicles beyond the parking area.

Carlyle Abbott, in the 1860s, became a hero by lassoing survivors off the wrecked clipper ship, *Sea Nymph*. He was one of two brothers who owned a nearby ranch for which the lagoon was named.

There is actually a pair of lagoons separated by a narrow isthmus. It's possible to canoe here if you don't mind portaging. Swimming, weather permitting, is also something you may wish to try, but is never advised in the ocean. Too treacherous.

We chose to picnic where the little fresh water stream drains from the lower lagoon into a pool, then makes its way to the sea.

On the beach beyond, only one other person was in sight. We munched in silence, sipping white wine and smiling occasionally, enchanted by where we were and what we saw.

Later, Barbara and I tried fishing Abbott's. We sat patiently in sand, wondering whether or not there were trout or any other species in the fresh water.

Not a single strike, but indeed a worthwhile adventure anyway, one we won't soon forget. Why not try it some time?

Taken from Pierce Point Road, yellow lupine bushes dot the moors and the lagoons snake down to the sea. Pathway is on the left.

KEHOE BEACH

56

skirt the lagoon to a great white dune

K EHOE BEACH IS less than three miles beyond Abbott's Lagoon
and five-tenths of a mile west of Pierce Point Road on an easy
trail with lots to see. It's a fine place for a short or long outdoor
interlude.

Roadside parking is available for a few cars. Rustic restrooms are
to one side of the entrance and a sign states the distance to the beach.
Dogs on leash are permitted but no swimming or wading due to the
treacherous nature of the surf.

Right off, you're skirting a boggy area as the path curves westward. There are brush-covered rolling hills on either side as you follow
the trail skirting the marsh which blossoms into a beautiful reed-tufted
lagoon long before reaching the sea. An out-of-the way location with
not many folks around, particularly during the week, you've stepped
into a world of rustic simplicity.

The real surprise comes when the trail leads directly into a massive white sand dune — pure, clean, shoe-filling sugar-fine — an
unexpected delight. Beyond, breakers spread foam on hard wet sand.
A salt-tinged breeze bends the clumps of nearby dune grass.

Looking north toward McClure's Beach are formidable bluffs.
Hikers are advised to use extreme caution. Southward stretches more
beach than you can imagine. Actually, you're standing at the northern
extremity of Point Reyes Beach and it's entirely possible that you could

walk nearly all the way by beach to Point Reyes Lighthouse. You would need a day.

This long stretch goes by several names: Ten Mile, Eleven Mile, Twelve Mile and Great Beach. And they all suggest the expansive nature of this windswept, often foggy always intriguing seashore with unusual formations of driftwood offering shelter from sea breezes and perfect spots to picnic, relax or nap.

The beauty of Kehoe held us there longer than we anticipated. We returned slowly, impressed by the brave rugged wildflowers, the yellow lupine bushes plus the profusion of grasses, reeds, sedges and other riparian growth surrounding the lagoon.

Back at the car, we lingered, looking westward once more as we emptied pure white sand from our shoes...

Just beyond the huge white dune, facing the north end cliffs bent grass gives testament to the constancy of the wind. Lagoon is to the left, and the beach stretches south forever.

MC CLURE'S BEACH

57

steep trail, remote beach & a bubbling brook

TWO AND A HALF miles beyond Inverness on Sir Francis Drake highway, branch right on Pierce Point Road and drive nine miles to its end. There you'll find a paved parking area, toilets, a phone and a sign telling you it's six-tenths of a mile to McClure's Beach. This is also the trailhead for a ten mile loop to Tomales Point and back, out where the tule elk roam. Take your choice.

Either is an outdoor adventure you won't soon forget. Let's take the one to McClure's. The trail descends quite steeply down a growth covered ravine toward the open sea. As you wind along you wonder if there could possibly be any water beneath all that ground cover. In season, you'll see stunted California poppies, gumweed, morning glory, buckwheat, lizardtail and more.

As you approach the beach you suddenly discover that a stream has emerged from beneath the cover and is dancing along the rocks in spirited fashion singing a gurgly little tune.

Expect wind and salt-tinged air. Once you reach the beach and face Elephant Rock, respect the sea, particularly at high tide. Steep formidable bluffs at either end protect this mile long stretch of sand. At low tides, pools are abundant with sea life. Hefty breakers are almost always putting on a dazzling display of spray as they crash with force against rocks and cliffs.

Swimming is prohibited here for obvious reasons. Same with wading. This is a beautiful, dangerous surf, an intriguing place for a picnic, particularly on a reasonably calm day. No dogs allowed.

If the day's a bit breezy, seek out a driftwood log for protection and spread your lunch on a cloth behind it, relax and watch the sea, the birds, the surf, nature at its best.

When the time comes to leave, take it easy up the trail. You're bound to notice items you missed going down. As you pause to catch your breath, look back at the crashing surf, now hushed by distance. Ahead is the parking lot and your car. When you finally arrive, sit a moment and reflect how exhilarating — yet marvelously calming — the experience has been.

End of the steep sandy path to McClure's Beach, two walkers are almost there. Invisible stream, that bubbles forth on the sand, is in the ravine to the left.

POINT REYES BEACH

58

miles & miles of sand & surging surf

P OINT REYES BEACH is an extensive stretch of sand. In fact, it's also called Ten Mile Beach or Great Beach, which gives you some idea of its uninterrupted length.

The Pacific Ocean is seldom flat or calm along here. Rather, wild and rugged with salt-tinged winds that make for healthy, exhilarated breathing, it is an awesome sight.

This long ribbon of sand and surf is a good place to visit any time. There are north and south automobile entrances to parking lots off of Sir Francis Drake Highway. Don't plan on swimming or wading — too treacherous. But you can walk or run for miles, fish, collect odd pieces of driftwood, or just plain escape to the crashing cadence of breakers.

Winter storms can be savage and the fog gets so thick that visibility is zero. This contributed to many shipwrecks, even after the lighthouse was built in 1870. Local ranchers were known to participate in rescue operations when possible and were also abreast of salvage laws. The first Coast Guard life-saving station was located along here from 1888 to 1927.

North and south parking lots are located 2.5 miles apart. Take Sir Francis Drake out of Inverness, bypass Johnson's Oyster Farm Road on your left and keep going until signs indicate the north parking area on your right. Here you'll find water, restrooms and picnic tables. Pets on leash are permitted. The south lot has the same facilities.

A few years ago, we took a dear friend, visiting from England, out to West Marin sightseeing. We, of course, stopped at north parking lot for a view of the mighty Pacific.

It was windy that day but clear. We could see for miles in every direction. Bette stood for a moment by the split-rail fence. Then, without a word, removed her shoes and walked straight down to where the waves touched the sand. She waited until a swish of water crept between her toes. Moments later, with an ecstatic smile on her face, she returned to the car, windblown and sandy.

"I'll never forget that," she said.

Neither will you.

Center section of Ten Mile Beach which stretches endlessly, until blocked in the north by the jutting cliff separating Kehoe and McClure's, taken from the north parking lot.

DRAKE'S BEACH

the shifting sands of history

59

I
F YOU PREFER a generous dash of historical controversy mixed with your outdoor living, be sure to visit Drake's Beach.

There's a large paved parking area, the Kenneth C. Patrick visitor center, Drake's Beach Cafe, restrooms, picnic tables and grills. And a sweeping view of bay and beach you won't soon forget.

This is a great place for hikers, joggers, runners, waders, sunbathers, anglers, birders and historians. There are miles and miles to explore.

The Nova Albion plaque was placed there by the Sir Francis Drake Quadricentennial Committee of the Marin Coast Chamber of Commerce June 18, 1979, 420 years and one day after Francis Drake (this great navigator had not yet been knighted at that time) supposedly sailed his tired, beaten Golden Hinde into this bay seeking sanctuary and anchorage to repair the vessel.

After digesting all the available facts, you may become one who firmly believes Drake landed somewhere else! The evidence on both sides is substantial but non-conclusive so the controversy continues.

There are a number of plaques to read and the visitor center will furnish written material on Sir Francis Drake.

The great arc that constitutes Drake's Beach is usually less windy than the open ocean, the surf quieter. The sand here constantly shifts

140

with the tides and seasons. Rocky shelves visible one day may be completely covered with sand another.

There's so much to do and explore here you may be drawn back several times. Most outdoor lovers are.

To get to this vast, fascinating stretch of nature, take Sir Francis Drake Highway out of Inverness for 14 miles, bear left at the sign.

You may think the bay looks tranquil, isolated and far removed from any major historical controversy. Seems so to me. Yet the continuing debate does keep history vital and alive.

Some of the buildings and structures at Drake's Beach, looking inland. Parking lot to the left and the bay over the dunes behind you.

CHIMNEY ROCK

—————————————————————— 60

a clean sweep

WILL THE REAL Chimney Rock please stand? Which one are you?

This is a question that naturally surfaces when you visit the historic spot near Point Reyes Lighthouse. Looking eastward from bluffs above the old Coast Guard station, several rocks jut from the sea, none really resembling a chimney. More disconcerting, there's a small, unusual outcropping as you bear left off Sir Francis Drake highway where the road forks.

"That looks like a chimney," I said to my wife.

"Can't be the real one," she replied.

It wasn't. Later we took the question of the rock's identity to Don Neubacher, chief of visitor services, Point Reyes National Seashore. "We've been asked a million times," he said. "Looking east, it's the largest rock."

So Chimney does stand tall, unannounced and proud without much resemblance to its title, yet still contributing to a worthwhile outdoor experience when you visit the complex named after it.

A narrow strip of blacktop leads left from Sir Francis Drake. Drive carefully. Soon you'll come to a paved parking area with a latrine and a trail heading to a a high bluff.

There are spectacular views from almost everywhere here. Below, commercial fishing boats bob at anchor to Drakes Bay's gentle swells.

Beyond are the white cliffs of Nova Albion. A road closed to vehicles winds down to a pier where this day a lone angler tried his luck. The lifeguard station beyond was moved from Point Reyes Beach to this more sheltered spot beneath the bluff in 1927 and eventually closed in 1968.

The two-story building is now an educational facility and working museum. Upstairs, in the renovated dormitory, educational groups, by appointment, can stay overnight.

On the last Sunday of the month, the facility is open to the public, 2 to 4 p.m., to view the exhibits and see slide presentations. Call (415) 663-8522 for more information.

Chimney Rock is the pointed one just offshore. At low tide it's possible to walk out to it. This taken from end of a path at the overlook before you get to the parking area. Bluff at left can be reached on a trail that starts at the lot.

POINT REYES LIGHTHOUSE

down 30-stories worth of stairs

F OR THOSE WHO prefer exercise along with their other outdoor activities, a visit to Marin's famed Point Reyes Lighthouse is a must. Although this is the foggiest spot on the Pacific Coast, there are plenty of clear, windy days to make the adventure an exhilarating experience.

A short side trip to the sea lion overlook near the parking lot is worthwhile. You can usually see or hear the animals far below and the view is superb.

It's four tenths of a mile from the paved parking area to the light-house proper with rugged terrain on all sides. The road is steep to begin with then levels off under windbent cypress trees before bypass-ing personnel living quarters.

At the top, just beyond the visitor's center, is a fenced overlook with large informative displays to add to your pleasure. Here the view is spectacular, awesome. A long ribbon of beach stretches northward while the restless Pacific Ocean pounds the rocky shoreline far below. Understandably, this is one of the most popular whale-watching spots anywhere January through March.

Now you begin the long descent on a cement stairway and path to the historic lighthouse, a distance equivalent to a 30 story building. There are three rest stations for the climb out.

The old light, imported from France in 1870, was reflected by over 1,000 pieces of glass and could be seen on clear nights 24 nautical miles at sea.

At intervals a park ranger explains the complex machinery connected with the light's operation.

To get to this fascinating, rugged point of land, follow Sir Francis Drake Highway all the way to its very end 16 miles beyond Inverness.

Regulations prohibit dogs and you must stay on established trails. Surrounding cliffs are extremely hazardous. Besides the visitor center and lighthouse, you'll find water, parking and restrooms. For further information call (415) 669-1534.

Down 30 stories worth of stairs to the lighthouse, taken from the top, a walk you won't soon forget. Views from this windiest foggiest spot on the Pacific Coast are spectacular— when visible!

Bon Tempe Lake from top of Mount Tamalpais

—— FURTHER READING ON MARIN ——

Arnot, Phil and Elvira Monroe: EXPLORING POINT REYES, A GUIDE TO POINT REYES NATIONAL SEASHORE, World Wide Publishing, Revised edition, 1983 — 5x6, 146 pages, maps, photographs, directory.

Arnot, Phil, POINT REYES: SECRET PLACES & MAGIC MOMENTS, World Wide Publishing/Tetra, Revised Edition 1988 — 5-1/2x8-1/2, 204 pages, photographs and maps by author, personal text sharing the mystical and private side of Point Reyes.

Arrigoni, Patricia: MAKING THE MOST OF MARIN: A CALIFORNIA GUIDE, Photography by Michael Bry, Presidio Press, 1981, — 5-1/2x8-1/2, 281 pages, photographs, maps, restaurant guide. Complete coverage and accurate text makes this a perfect reference book.

Dunham, Tacy: DISCOVER MARIN STATE PARKS, HIKING WEST MARIN, MARIN BIKE PATHS, MARIN HEADLANDS TRAIL GUIDE, GGNRA, NATURE WALKS FOR CHILDREN, WANDERING MARIN TRAILS, a delightful series of small 5-1/2x8-1/2 books, illustrated by Troy Dunham, with detailed maps, line drawings, and pertinent information well presented.

Fairley, Lincoln: MOUNT TAMALPAIS, A HISTORY, Picture editor, James Heig, Scottwall Associates, 1987, — 8-1/2x11, 202 pages, photographs, maps, fascinating and comprehensive text.

Geary, Ida: MARIN TRAILS; A NATURAL HISTORY GUIDE TO MARIN COUNTY, Tamal Land Press, 1969, — 6x6, 102 pages, original plant prints by author, delightful and surprisingly undated text - (which shows the comparative permanency of the great outdoors).

Hayden, Mike: PIER FISHING ON SAN FRANCISCO BAY; THE COMPLETE GUIDE TO PUBLIC PIERS AROUND SAN FRANCISCO BAY, Chronicle Books, 1982, 120 pages — 9x8, (Marin County "North Bay Piers" — pages 70, 77), photographs, maps, line drawings of fish, cooking hints.

Martin, Don and Kay: MT. TAM; A HIKING, RUNNING AND NATURE GUIDE, Martin Press, 1986, 100 pages — 5-1/2x8-1/2, excellent maps for each place, seasonal guide, geology, history, wildflowers, an excellent reference book.

Taber, Tom: DISCOVERING SAN FRANCISCO BAY, Oak Valley Press, 1978, 128 pages — 5-1/2x8-1/2, photographs, maps, line drawings, (Marin County, pages 88 through, 104), excellently done.

Whitnah, Dorothy, AN OUTDOOR GUIDE TO THE SAN FRANCISCO BAY AREA; EXPLORING WITH BOOTS, BIKES, BACKPACKS, BUSES, BOATS, BOOKS AND BART, Wilderness Press, New Edition 1987, — 4-3/4x7-3/4, 364 pages, (Marin County — pages 45 -145), photographs, detailed maps, a format providing specific information on public transportation, facilities, etc. A fine reference book.

Whitnah, Dorothy: POINT REYES; A GUIDE TO THE TRAILS, ROADS, BEACHES, CAMPGROUNDS, LAKES, TREES, FLOWERS AND ROCKS OF POINT REYES NATIONAL SEASHORE, Wilderness Press, 1981, 114 pages — 6x9, maps, photographs, wildflowers, line drawings, precautions, clear concise text.

Wurm, Ted and Al Graves: THE CROOKEDEST RAILROAD IN THE WORLD; CALIFORNIA'S MT. TAMALPAIS & MUIR WOODS RAILROAD, Revised and enlarged, 1983, Interurbans Publications, 136 pages — 8-1/2x11, vintage photographs, memorabilia, line drawings of engines, maps and marvelous text.

MAPS

BAY EDGES — Prepared by the Institute for the Human Environment for the San Francisco Bay Conservation and Development Commission, 1981. WEST BAY - Bird's eye view topographical pictorial maps, give a wonderfully clear picture of terrain.

Recreational Map, POINT REYES NATIONAL SEASHORE, Erickson Maps, large foldout detailed map, orange cover, comprehensive.

Recreational Map, GOLDEN GATE NATIONAL RECREATION AREA, Erickson Maps, large folded map in an orange envelope, detailed, with listing of pertinent data about GGNRA. (Not as convenient to use as the foldout map, above)

INDEX OF PLACES

PICNIC AREAS

TRAILS

The Golden Gate Bridge from Fort Baker

Spillway at Lake Lagunitas after good rain

ABOUT THE MURDOCKS

It was Larry Green, KCBS Fisherman's Forecaster, who pointed Dick Murdock toward his second (third?) career — as an outdoor writer. Larry, a railfan and steam buff, knew Dick as a railroad author as well as a fishing buddy. When he learned the *San Rafael Independent Journal,* as it was titled then, would soon be in need of an outdoor columnist, he alerted Dick. "You can write, you can fish. Go for it," he said. Dick presented three sample columns. Six weeks later on September 2, 1981, his first outdoors piece appeared. The rest, as they say, is history. He now writes for several papers, averaging an impressive output of a column every other day and a half!

Dick, born in Oakland May 15, 1917, lived in Contra Costa county most of his adult life, working for Southern Pacific out of Oakland. Five years — 1951-1955 — were spent in Dunsmuir near Mount Shasta on steam engines, as chronicled in his popular book, *Smoke In The Canyon.*

It wasn't until 1972 that his eyes and his heart turned toward Marin when he fell in love with life-long Ross resident Jayne Rattray May, divorced mother of five. Jayne, a trained journalist, was then teaching grade school in Mill Valley, living in the home her parents had built in 1924 when she was five years old.

They were married there at a garden ceremony during the drought in February 1977. Already Dick and Jayne had pooled their impressive talents to produce his first book, *Walnut Creek's Unique Old Station.* Now they formed a small publishing company, MAY-MURDOCK PUBLICATIONS. Though both held demanding full-time jobs, in that year they published two books, *Port Costa 1879-1941* and *Love Lines,* excerpted from their years of courtship correspondence.

Dick retired from Southern Pacific after 37 years in engine service on Memorial Day 1978; Jayne left teaching after 15 years in the summer of 1980.

So what does 'retired' mean to this pair? Total involvement in numerous projects, organizations, activities and publications that keep them busier than ever. In search of stories and relaxation, they try to break away one week a month for travel in their *Adventurewagen,* a goal seldom reached.

Point Bonita to Point Reyes is the fourteenth book they've published. With **The Northwesterner — Fall 1988**, they have edited and designed the fourth issue of Northwestern Pacific Railroad Historical Society's magazine. Dick's twice weekly columns in the *Marin Independent Journal,* monthly writings in *Port Costa News,* and bi-weekly in *Fish Sniffer,* are constant deadlines.

Jayne has remained involved with Friends of Hospice since her mother's care by Hospice of Marin in 1976. Both are active in Toastmasters International, Dick with the rank of Able Toastmaster. He and Jayne lead seminars throughout the Bay area on such varied subjects as railroads, fishing and publishing.

The Murdocks are a true literary team doing everything on their respective books except typesetting and actual printing. They serve as editor and critic of each others' work. Jayne does most of the photography and design, and they share time, more or less graciously, on the computer. Gathering information for columns, doing outdoor research, getting away for mini-vacations in their *Adventurewagen,* keeping up with their ever-expanding family (13th grandchild due just as this goes to press!) fills to overflowing their time.

Several books are in the planning stage, sitting patiently on the back burner, rail excursions are scheduled, plans made well into the next year. And the next! Life for these two is never dull.

ACKNOWLEDGMENTS

To all who answered questions and shared their specialized expertise: Leo Cronin who knows the county's creeks; Don Neubacher for seashore information; Ruth Williamson, photographic advice and support; Clif Rattenbury, color photo work for the cover.

To those who checked the manuscript for current accuracy and did incidental proofreading: John Sansing, Gail Lester, Eric McGuire, Ron Stephens, and Kent Diehl. To Greig Shepard for final proofing.

To George Epperson, expert on Sir Francis Drake, for searching out an appropriate quote to grace the dedication page.

To Jill Thomas, at R. Nolan & Sons, who helped so much with the page design.

And to Dr. Sanjay Sakhuja, Angela Noel and others of Krishna Copy for beyond-the-call-of-duty attention to our typesetting and cover needs...etc. etc. etc.

Thank you all.

COLOPHON

Typesetting: Krishna Copy Center, 66 Kearny Street, San Francisco, CA using Kurzweil Optical Scanner, Macintosh II and the Linotronic 300

Typeface: Text, Garamond Light; Headings, Universe Bold & Light; Initial caps: Avant Garde

Paper: 60# Glatfelter Spring Forge white

Cover photograph: Clif Rattenbury, San Anselmo, CA

Color separation: Image Arts, 919 Filley Street, Lansing, MI

Printing & binding: Thomson-Shore, Inc. 7300 West Joy Road, Dexter MI

MAY-MURDOCK PUBLICATIONS
Drawer 1346 - 90 Glenwood Avenue
Ross CA 94957-1346 - (415) 454-1771

RAILROAD BOOKS BY DICK MURDOCK

SMOKE IN THE CANYON: My Steam Days in Dunsmuir
144 pages, 63 historical photographs,   hard cover $26.00
original artwork by Charles Endom   perfect bound   16.00

PORT COSTA 1879-1941: A Saga of Sails, Sacks and Rails
40 pages, historical photographs,
original artwork by Charles Endom   saddle stitched   6.00

HOGHEADS & HIGHBALLS: Railroad Lore and Humor
64 pages, sketches by Charles Endom   perfect bound   5.00

LOVE AFFAIR WITH STEAM
40 pages,   saddle stitched   3.00

EARLY CALL FOR THE PERISHABLES, A Day at the Throttle
24 pages,   saddle stitched   2.00

WALNUT CREEK'S UNIQUE OLD STATION
24 pages, 17 photographs   saddle stitched   2.00

BOOKS BY JAYNE MURDOCK

I PAINTED ON A BRIGHT RED MOUTH: The War Years
December 1941-August 1945
64 pages, vintage photo-collages   perfect bound   5.00

UNTIL DEATH AND AFTER: How To Live With A Dying Intimate
64 pages   perfect bound   4.00

BRIEF INFINITY: A Love Story in Haiku
64 pages   perfect bound   4.00

LOVE LINES: A True Love Story in Lyric Prose
by Jayne May & Dick Murdock, 134 pages   perfect bound   5.00

OTHER OFFERINGS BY MAY-MURDOCK

SHANNON: WHAT'S IT ALL MEAN? 101 commentaries
        by Wayne Shannon, 128 pages   perfect bound   6.00

THE NORTHWESTERNER — Twice yearly slick magazine of
        the Northwestern Pacific Railroad Historical
        Society, vintage photos, articles by well-known
        railroad writers.
        PREMIERE ISSUE — 1987, 24 pages, WINTER
        1987-1988, 28 pages, SPRING 1988, 28 pages,
        FALL 1988, 32 pages   each issue   5.00

SEND FOR FREE BROCHURE
MONEY BACK GUARANTEE ON ALL MAY-MURDOCK PUBLICATIONS

Outcropping at top of Mt. Tamalpais

Point Bonita Lighthouse

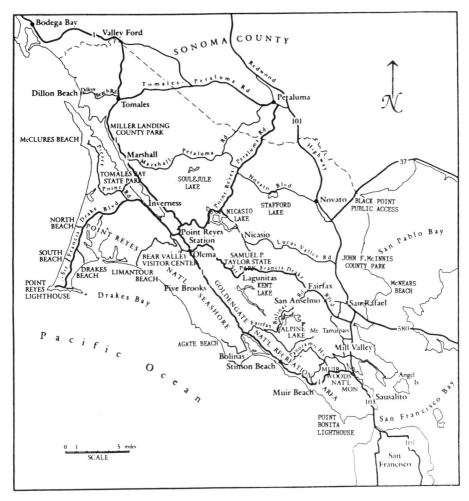

Map by Dewey Livingston